THE ACID TEST

THE AUTOBIOGRAPHY OF
CLYDE BEST

THE ACID TEST

THE AUTOBIOGRAPHY OF CLYDE BEST

Clyde Best

✦ deCoubertin
B O O K S

THE ACID TEST

THE AUTOBIOGRAPHY OF
CLYDE BEST

With Andrew Warshaw

deCoubertin
B O O K S

First Edition

deCoubertin Books, Studio N, Baltic Creative Campus, Liverpool, L1 OAH
www.decoubertin.co.uk

ISBN: 978-1-909245-36-5
Special Edition ISBN: 978-1-909245-45-7

A CIP catalogue record for this book is available from the British Library.
Cover design by Allen Mohr.
Special Edition cover by MilkyOne Creative; Illustration by Steve Welsh/ Miniboro
Typeset by Sabahat Muhammed.
Printed and bound by Standart.

This book is dedicated to my family for their love and support over the years during my wonderful football journey.

CONTENTS

FOREWORD

BY HARRY REDKNAPP

I REMEMBER THE FIRST TIME I EVER CLAPPED EYES ON CLYDE BEST as if it was yesterday. It was at West Ham's training pitch at Chadwell Heath. His coach had written a letter to Ron Greenwood recommending Clyde for a trial. The senior players had just finished training and looked across at this huge lad who was only sixteen but looked more like twenty-four as he trained with the youth team. While most of the kids were practising their crossing and smashing shots over the bar, Clyde was having none of that as he took a cross on his chest and volleyed the ball into the top corner. Everyone was amazed and Ron, who was in charge of the first team, went over to have a look and was immediately impressed. That was the beginning of a special bond between Clyde and West Ham United Football Club.

When you look back, it is impossible to overestimate the impact Clyde had, not only on the club but also on English football generally and society as a whole. You'd have to put him right at the top in terms of breaking down racial barriers. There were precious few black players and there, suddenly, was this kid who had come all the way from Bermuda to take his chance. You will read later on about how Clyde became part of the Charles family (mother Jessie and her mixed-race West Ham boys John and Clive). They really looked after him. They needed to. It wasn't the most salubrious of environments, in fact it was a tough area. But they were wonderful to Clyde and he adored them.

Not long after Clyde joined, the West Ham squad went over to the United

States on tour and finished up in Bermuda. We had Geoff Hurst, Bobby Moore and Martin Peters, our three World Cup-winning West Ham stars, with us, but when we touched down at Bermuda airport, the only person the crowd were interested in was their own boy who had, if you like, come home even though he had only been away a short while. That's how much of a hero he was, even as a teenager.

But then who could be surprised? Clyde was always a class act, a real gentleman. All of us players loved him. He wasn't really into drinking or partying yet he enjoyed a night out, adapted well to the East End culture and became one of the gang. More than that, he won over the hearts of the fans.

Let's be honest, it wasn't easy for him. Everywhere he went he took abuse. What he had to go through was hurtful to all of us because he was such a special fellow, a laid-back guy who didn't have a bad bone in him. He was a real pioneer, a gentle giant who not only had great ability but a strong determination to make it in English football. How many people would swap the pink sands of Hamilton for Canning Town? What he left behind was paradise, which perhaps explains his mentality. Nothing was going to stand in his way of becoming a successful footballer. He treated racism with the contempt it deserved.

I had some great times with Clyde. My only regret is that perhaps he left the club too early. But one thing's for sure. These days, there are so many fantastic black players but they all owe a huge debt to Clyde. He was English football's first real black role model. To adapt as he did was truly incredible. How he didn't run home after two weeks, after leaving behind that lifestyle, I just don't know. It showed incredible character.

When the world mourned the death of Muhammad Ali, the only footballer I thought could come close to 'The Greatest' was Clyde. Talk about battling through adversity. Respect, mate.

HARRY REDKNAPP, JUNE 2016

PROLOGUE

MORE THAN FORTY YEARS AGO SOMETHING HAPPENED WHICH, when I think back, still sends a shiver down my spine. Perhaps because it was so shocking, I've shied away from talking about it. Speaking out then might have made me even more of a target; after all, things were very different back in the 1970s. It was a hostile time, a time when racism was endemic in English football. I was still young, a teenager, and living in digs at the home of Jessie Charles (mother of John and Clive, of whom much more later).

The 1970/71 season had been under way for a few weeks and one Friday we all had our mail brought down to the dressing room, as you used to do in those days. Usually it was all complimentary stuff, fans asking for autographs and things like that. But as I sifted through it, one letter, written anonymously, made my blood run cold. It warned me that as soon as I emerged from the tunnel and took the field the following day, I would have acid thrown in my eyes.

I can't remember who the opposition were that day but that's irrelevant. To say it knocked me sideways is an understatement. I'd had plenty of stick when we played away from home about the colour of my skin. I'll never forget going to Everton on one occasion and hearing perpetual monkey chants. I knew who they were directed at. After all, I was a novelty. Most people had never seen a black player before. I also knew the best way to silence the perpetrators. I picked the ball up on the halfway line with an Everton player, Terry Darracott, hanging on to my shirt, trying to pull me down. I dragged him literally all the way to the penalty area and when the keeper came out I sold him a dummy and clipped it over his head. After the game Joe Royle, who later went on to become Everton manager, came up to me and said it was the best goal ever seen at Goodison Park. It was my way of making a statement.

But this was different. This was not something I could just shrug off in my usual way. It was a shock to the system but it was important to me that my team-mates never knew about it. Nor any of my friends outside the game. The only person who knew was Ron Greenwood, my manager. Ron had become a father figure to me at West Ham. He had always tried to keep the press away from me to stop me getting too exposed at too young an age. When I handed the acid warning letter to him, he remained utterly calm, hiding it away in a draw and telling me not to worry. I don't know to this day what happened to it. Ron had a wonderful way of putting his players at ease, yet despite his reassurance I hardly slept that night.

I thought about telling my family but I was far away from my homeland of Bermuda and, anyway, it would have only worried them. I also thought about telling Bobby Moore, who was my captain. Bobby was a special guy and I played with him right up until he went to Fulham in 1974. He was so genuine, one of the best human beings I have ever met in my life. His death in 1993 at the age of 51 came far too early. I always appreciated the fact that he used to take me aside and quietly tell me what I needed to do. I seriously thought of telling him about the letter but it was something that I had to deal with myself personally. With Ron Greenwood being the manager I decided he would be the one to go and tell.

Having said that, it wouldn't surprise me at all if he told Bobby next day at the game, just in case something happened on the field. Ron may also, for all I know, have told some of the other senior players but I never found out. No one ever said anything to me – and I didn't ask. As I say, it was something I had to try and cope with on my own. That's just the kind of person I was – and still am. I had encountered racist chants before but never anything like this. Who could have sent such a letter? Surely not a West Ham fan. I got on brilliantly with everyone at the club, on and off the field, at least until late in my career when my form dropped and a small minority turned against me. But someone, somewhere, obviously bore a grudge against me because of the colour of my skin. Although I don't know who, if any, among the players knew about it,

Ron obviously told the directors and some of the administration staff because I know for a fact that the police were informed. When kick-off came a phalanx of security personnel formed a cordon on both sides of the tunnel. That was my protection, so to speak, but I was still scared as hell, thinking to myself, 'If you're going to throw acid at me, please don't mess with my face. Throw it at my arms if you have to but, please, not my face.'

I can tell you, I have never run so fast in my life for ninety minutes. I just couldn't stand still, I had to keep moving. It was as if I had been threatened by an assassin who was planning to hunt me down and finish me off. At the end of the game, the police formed another cordon around the tunnel and I went straight through the middle. I can't imagine what my team-mates or the fans – who were all oblivious to this threat – must have thought was going on. Only once I got to the dressing room afterwards did I realise nothing was going to happen to me. Talk about a sigh of relief. I had come through unscathed.

This is probably the first time any of my former team-mates, if they are reading this, will know about the incident. But I can tell you it was the worst experience of my life, at least as far as racism is concerned. You always had taunts from the terraces but to get something in writing like this felt so much more real. I couldn't just say, 'I'm not going to play'; I had to play through it. Some people might wonder if the letter was genuine but I have no doubt it was. You could tell by the writing and the spelling. It was someone who knew what they were doing, that's for sure. But I never knew where it came from because I never even looked at the postmark. I gave it straight to Ron once I saw the contents.

However, I understood immediately what the motive was. West Ham were one of the first clubs to include black players – well before West Brom unveiled their so-called Three Degrees (Cyrille Regis, Laurie Cunningham and Brendan Batson). The letter hurt me because everyone at West Ham had a certain mentality. It was a working-class environment and everyone had a healthy respect for one another, from the tea ladies to the groundsmen. I couldn't imagine anyone could be so prejudiced as to physically threaten me in that way. It was especially shocking because, as I say, I'd never encountered such hostility before – and never felt threatened in the same way thereafter, although there were the odd idiots hurling abuse.

Since retiring, I've had countless people ask me how I managed to deal with racism in general. My answer is that I was not just making a stand for myself but for every black player who has played the game, not just then but ever since. Throughout my career, the spectre of racism was never far away, but I had to try and be bigger than the bigots. I was determined not to be thrown off my game because I knew that if I let that happen, my team would effectively be one player short. I needed to let the people who had paid good money to support West Ham know that I had come here to do business.

Do I wish I had been playing in an era when racism was less prevalent in football? Not really. I believe everyone is here for a purpose. I honestly believe I was chosen to do what I had to do at the time. Which was to fly the flag for non-white players. When you look at how many black people were playing in England at the time, it wasn't that many. Before televised games started, nobody except those who went to games even knew that black players were involved. Once television coverage exploded, people like myself were given exposure. A lot of players over the years have come up to me and thanked me for making it possible for them to get somewhere.

But did the racism prevent me playing longer in England? That's a different question. Psychologically, possibly yes; because no human being wants to be beaten down like that. Not that any actual players ever verbally abused me. I can't say it didn't happen under their breath, but I can't recall anyone doing it to my face. No, I tell I lie. There was one incident when I was playing a reserve game at Upton Park (also known as the Boleyn Ground because of its association with Anne Boleyn) against Norwich when a Canaries player – I really can't remember who it was – made a comment. The blood rushed to my head and I hit him so hard in a shoulder-to-shoulder challenge that I knocked him into the stands. That was my payback, if you like. But I need to add here that I was rarely, if ever, racially abused away from the terraces. Walking the streets, never. Taking the underground, never.

I'VE THOUGHT LONG AND HARD ABOUT WHY I WANTED TO write this book. I guess it all comes down to telling it like it was: what I had to go through to fulfil my ambitions. It certainly wasn't an easy path that I took.

No black player would ever make it in England, they used to say. We couldn't take the bad weather, the heavy pitches. Well, we proved them wrong on that score, didn't we? But racism was personal. I've lost count of the number of times team-mates came up to me over the years and said: 'Clyde, I don't know how you coped with that. Rather you than me.'

And it wasn't just footballers who had to put up with the abuse. Black hospital nurses, black teachers, black shopkeepers. You name it, all of us had to deal with it. I will make many references in this book to the influence my dad had on me. I make no apologies for that. He said I owed it to everyone to make a go of my career, that what I was doing would serve as a barometer for generations to come. If I could make it better for black people coming into the game, that was success enough in itself. I honestly believe I was chosen to play football and I thank my parents for teaching me how to deal with people. At first, perhaps, I wasn't aware of the battles and challenges I would have to face, but I think I did a pretty good job of it. I always remember my ma saying, 'Treat people the way you want to be treated. Then you can't go wrong in life.' She was right. Let's face it, you are always going to find people who don't know you from Adam but just don't like you. You can't let that affect you. You just have to move on.

When I switch on the television nowadays and see so many black players and realise how much I had to do with what is now considered the norm, that is my real victory – just as important as winning games and scoring goals. When you think of all the abuse that was going on in my day, it's remarkable that we have got where we are in terms of multiracial tolerance. Not everywhere, of course. In some parts of Europe, it seems no lessons have been learned at all. But in Britain, thank goodness, players are no longer judged by the colour of their skin. Well, for the most part anyway . . .

I'm not sure, however, whether the same can be said about managers. I'd like to think the same applies, but there has got to be a reason why there are so few black coaches. I don't want to believe it has anything to do with racism. Maybe owners of clubs just don't have the trust in appointing black managers. Perhaps someone should ask them what the reason is. I think eventually it's a process we are going to have to go through, since it's not what it should be. It's something we should all question. After all, football belongs to everybody.

EARLY DAYS

I WAS BORN CLYDE CYRIL BEST ON 24 FEBRUARY 1951 IN BERMUDA, a tiny island of only 20 square miles – and some wonderful pink-sand beaches – located about 600 miles off the coast of North Carolina in the Atlantic Ocean. Many think that Bermuda is in the Caribbean, although it is actually about 1,000 miles north of the Bahamas. The geographic proximity to the United States has led to a distinctive blend of British and American culture but we are proud of our British heritage. Some 500 years ago, Spanish explorer Juan de Bermudez discovered what was then an isolated archipelago, which was subsequently named after him – even though he made no attempt to land. In the early seventeenth century British colonists arrived and in 1620 we became a self-governing colony. We have a pretty diversified community with numerous nationalities and ethnic groups. Around 55 per cent of Bermudians are of African descent, as many people in this part of the world are. While we try to stand on our own two feet, I don't think many of us would like to be truly independent of Britain. Don't forget, in 1995 we had our own referendum over whether Bermuda should become an independent sovereign state or remain a British Dependent Territory. Roughly three-quarters of the turnout voted against independence.

We're pretty blessed compared to most parts of the world. Bermuda is a picturesque place with a great climate most of the year. Summer means fishing, scuba diving and water skiing, depending on your interests. The pace of life is perfect for relaxation. It's a far cry from the 100mph roller-coaster life of, say, London. As I would discover several years later.

While being very much a Bermudian, I have strong connections with Barbados. The two islands may be around 1,300 miles apart – almost three hours' flying time north to south, although these days you can't fly direct and have to travel via New York – but a part of me will always have a strong affinity with Barbados for one very powerful reason. My father, Joseph Nathaniel Best, was born in St Michael's, Barbados, the eldest of four children. Dad was a firm believer in working hard and attended Wesley Hall Boys' School in Bridgetown, the island's capital. After leaving Wesley, he enrolled in correspondence courses before joining the merchant navy.

The Second World War began just before Dad's twentieth birthday. He was in the merchant navy at the time, working on a ship called *Lady Drake*, owned by the Canadian National Steamship Company. There were five such vessels in the company, all named after a British admiral: *Lady Drake* after Sir Francis Drake; *Lady Somers* after Admiral Sir George Somers (who was shipwrecked in Bermuda in 1609); *Lady Hawkins* after Sir John Hawkins; *Lady Nelson* after Admiral Horatio Nelson and *Lady Rodney* after Admiral Sir George Rodney. The flotilla of ships plied a route from the St Lawrence Seaway in Canada, all the way down the east coast of the United States to Bermuda, then into the Caribbean.

When he left the merchant navy, Dad took a job in the Royal Naval Dockyard in Bermuda, a massive fortification at the western end of the island. The dockyard housed every piece of equipment imaginable for Royal Navy ships: warehouses, workshops, armament stores, galleys, administrative offices. Someone once told me that the Royal Engineers who built the Bermuda dockyard laid it out in exactly the same way as the dockyards in Malta, Gibraltar, Hong Kong and Singapore – right down to the gates and sentry boxes. Little did Dad know how much it would play in the *footballing* life of one of his children!

Dad met my mother, Dorothy Pauline Smith, while he was working in the dockyard and they were married on 12 September 1942 in St James' church in Somerset in the northwest of Bermuda, located in Sandys Parish. This was at the height of the U-boat menace in the Atlantic and Caribbean, when millions of tons of shipping were being sunk by the German submarines. My father's brother, Cyril, who has lived in Canada since emigrating in the mid-1960s to work as a welding technician a few years before I left for England, can still remember as a child in Barbados seeing flames engulf oil tankers torpedoed in Caribbean waters on the horizon. He lived close to the beach and says German submarines were all around.

The very same day as he was married, my dad sailed from Bermuda to Trinidad, where he enlisted in the Royal Naval Volunteer Reserve. He served in corvettes and other escort vessels for the duration of the war and was awarded the Atlantic Star and Victory medals by the War Office. Afterwards he returned to be with his new family and resumed work at the dockyard, though we never quite knew what he actually did. I wasn't even born at the time and it's a bit of a gap in the family annals. As far as I was concerned as a small child, he was in the prison service. That's the profession he was in when I was growing up and where he stayed for 26 years, working his way up from a basic officer to deputy commissioner.

My parents moved into a house on Beacon Hill Road in Sandys Parish and that's where I was born six years after the war ended. Bermuda is divided into parishes, all named after investors in the original Somers Isles Company during the seventeenth century. Also known as the Company of the Somers Isles or the London Company of the Somers, it was formed in 1615 to explore and colonise Bermuda, before being dissolved in 1684.

We have no rivers or mountains in Bermuda, no sources of fresh running water. The roofs of our houses are limewashed to collect rainwater, which is funnelled into a tank beneath our houses, then pumped back inside for showers and washing. Our houses are painted in different pastel colours of blue, pink and yellow. Tourists to Bermuda always exclaim at the beauty of the island and the prettiness of our cottages with their white roofs.

My brothers Bobby and Carlton, and my sisters Mae, Marie and Eileen, had all already been born so little Clyde, eventually one of eight siblings, had lots of attention from everyone when he was brought home from the maternity ward of King Edward VII Memorial Hospital. Tragically, my eldest brother Bobby died when he was only 36. He'd had diabetes all his life and in those days it was harder to treat than today. I'll never forget returning from England for the funeral during my time at West Ham, then having to get back for the following Saturday to play Liverpool. All the energy had drained out of me what with the travelling and the whole emotional experience of it all. We all have such fond memories of Bobby and, to make matters worse, his daughter, my niece, died of cancer around thirteen years ago. I guess the family has suffered its fair share of tragedy, but that's the unpredictable thing about life. You just never know what's around the corner. Nothing is forever.

*

SOMERSET IS A VERY CLOSE-KNIT COMMUNITY. MY PARENTS enrolled me in West End Primary in 1955 where my teacher, Miss Lovette Brown, was waiting for me that first September day. I enjoyed school. My father had instilled a strong work ethic in me, something I have carried with me all my life. He insisted I work hard and play hard in everything I did, whether it be schoolwork or football or cricket.

My primary school years seemed to flash by. From Miss Brown's class (primary one) I progressed quickly through primary two with Mrs Manders then primary three with Mrs Bassett – and I was playing football every spare minute. In fact, I can't remember a time in my life when I didn't – until my retirement. When I was only six I used to play in Big Boys against Small Boys matches. Anyone who couldn't keep possession had to leave the game. I was learning fast. I remember some of the players to this day: Bernard George, Randolph Brangman, Gene Riley, Gregory and Gordon Gilbert, Clifford Russell, and my brother Carlton.

While I was still at primary school my family moved to Hog Bay. Tourists who come to Bermuda today regard Hog Bay beach as one of the secrets of the island, mainly because it's only really a beach at low tide, maybe four hours a day. I wasn't interested in sunbathing. It was purely football, and shortly after we moved I found other friends to play with like Winslow and Robert Dill, Tommy and John Harvey, Robert and Mel Roberts. It's remarkable what you retain in the memory as a footballer, and what you don't. As you can see, I can name all these kids I kicked a ball around with yet, because of the pace of life later on, I lost track of a load of things that happened to me and have wracked my brains to share it all with you. I guess one's earliest memories are often those that stick in the mind for the longest.

The Harvey brothers had another brother who played for local team Somerset Eagles. We used to go and watch them on Sundays. The Eagles were coached by Gladstone Burchall, a forward-thinking strategist who ended up going to the UK to study coaching methods. Guess where he went? Right first time . . . West Ham. That was my first introduction to the famous claret and blue. As a nine-year-old I could never imagine that one day I would wear their famous strip.

I was still playing regularly for West End Primary and I can remember the very first trophy I won when we defeated Central School 4–2 in the final of the Primary Schools Cup, the first time our school had ever won it.

I was quickly growing up. Everything in Somerset was close at hand – my school, my friends, my football. But nothing lasts forever and after primary seven I transferred to secondary school. For the first time in my life I had to leave secure, comfortable surroundings and travel by bus to my new school, which was half the length of Bermuda away, right in the middle of the island.

My secondary school was named after one of Great Britain's most iconic leaders – Sir Winston Churchill. Our principal was Ivor Cunningham who, like my father, had been born in the West Indies. I loved my time at Churchill, also known as Prospect Boys. I was taught from an early age about discipline. If you didn't behave you got caned. I think it only happened to me a couple of times, once when I was about twelve, but that's all it took for me to pay attention! One particular occasion still annoys me to this day. Two boys were having a fight and I thought about taking the initiative and stepping in to stop it. I didn't, they got caught and – to make his point that the school wouldn't stand for this sort of thing – the principal took the strap to the whole class. Unfair maybe, but that's what happened. If I'd intervened and stopped it, no one would have known about it. Well, not the teachers anyway. It's no fun being caned, let me tell you. It taught me from an early age to be a leader, not a follower. I wasn't prepared to take the rap for something I hadn't done.

I met some wonderful people at school, many of whom are still friends. If I had a favourite subject it was probably geography or history, but nothing came close to playing sport, which prepares you for life. The thing about sport is that it teaches you to be a team player, so than when you are in the workforce, it helps you get on better with people. I see a lot of people today who are not happy in their jobs. When I ask them if they have ever played sport, the answer is invariably no.

All of a sudden I was playing football with boys of the same age as myself who had come from other primary schools all over Bermuda. Just like my primary team, I can still remember Churchill's under-13 team: Sheldon Bradshaw, Larry Brangman, Shirley Nusum, Clarence Symonds, David Frost, Richard Simmons, Dale Russell, James Parsons, Courtland Furbert, Milton Jones, Erskine (Cho) Smith, Roger Hunt, David Furbert, Cecille Tucker, Damon Simmons. The names may not mean much to you but to me they were an integral part of my sporting upbringing. Especially Clarence Symonds.

Clarence and I played virtually from day one at elementary school all the way to local club level. He was with me all through my early development. The two of us used to go round carol singing at Christmas to raise enough money to buy our first set of footballing jerseys. I played with Clarence until I went to England, and with Sheldon Bradshaw. They used to call us the three musketeers. Like me, the two of them are both retired now. Clarence used to work for Cable and Wireless, while Sheldon had a career in construction.

We soon began to make a name for ourselves in the Bermuda secondary schools league, and were coached by some of the best staff on the island. We didn't just beat other teams – we thrashed them. In fact, we won every age-group we played in: under-13, over-13, under-15, over-15. We won every cup that was up for grabs and I don't think we ever lost a game – league or cup – during all the time I was at Churchill. And we didn't just win by the odd goal either. I remember scoring sixteen – yes, sixteen – goals in one particular game. That's got to be some kind of record, surely?

2

IT COULD HAVE BEEN CRICKET

ALTHOUGH MY FIRST LOVE WAS ALWAYS FOOTBALL, I WAS playing cricket from an early age too, representing Churchill at school level as well as Somerset Cricket Club, where I played as an all-rounder at the ripe old age of thirteen, even though the average age was nineteen or twenty. I was big for my age – taller and broader than most of the other kids at around 5ft 8in and around eight stone – though I'd like to think it also had something to do with talent.

The one cricket game in Bermuda that is religiously followed is what we call simply 'Cup Match', the annual fixture between one end of the island and the other – Somerset versus St George's. It's so popular a two-day holiday is taken, which is surely unique anywhere in the world. The island literally shuts down. Every year, before the start of the Cup Match holiday, rival fans can be seen donning their team's colours – red and navy for Somerset, pale blue and dark blue for St George's – in preparation for the big event. The venue for the game changes yearly as each side takes a turn in hosting.

The forerunner to Cup Match was introduced after the abolition of slavery in Bermuda. Men from Somerset and St George's met in friendly rivalry and held celebrations of emancipation by holding annual picnics, the highlight of which was a friendly cricket match played between lodges from the east and west ends of the island. In 1901, during a match between two major Friendly Societies, an agreement was made to play for an annual trophy. The following year a silver cup was awarded and Cup Match was officially born. Yet it embraces so much more than cricket. Emancipation Day symbolises one of the most significant moments in our history. It acknowledges a period in our history that shaped and continues to influence our society today. It is a time for reflection and rejoicing. It is a time for assessment, self-improvement and for planning the future. When slavery was abolished we moved closer to the ideals of bringing our island community together.

To this day I am the youngest person ever to compete in 'Cup Match', playing for Somerset when I was just fifteen. I played a second time a couple of years later but by then I had decided to choose football. If I'm honest, my dad would probably have preferred me to stay with cricket. I have strong memories of visiting Barbados with my father when they gained their independence in 1966. I was fifteen at the time and the West Indies were the most exciting cricket team in the world, packed with flair and flamboyance, dash and daring. My dad had grown up with the three Ws – Worrell, Weekes and Walcott – and was so keen for me to play professionally, he introduced me to Everton Weekes. I remember being in total awe of the guy. It was the cricketing equivalent of meeting Pelé. Which I also did further down the road. All three Ws were born within seventeen months of each other and within a mile of Kensington Oval in Barbados. With a test average of 58.61, Everton was regarded by many as the closest post-war batsman in style to Don Bradman.

Everton, or rather Sir Everton as he later became, retired from Test cricket in 1958 due to a persistent thigh injury but continued in the first-class game until 1964. At the time of our visit, he was coaching in schools and offered to coach me if I came to play in Barbados. The mere thought of it gave me goose bumps. Clyde Best coached by Everton Weekes! Had that happened, I may well have ended up as an international cricketer. I knew my dad secretly wanted me to take up Everton's offer, even though he didn't tell me to my face. I could just read his mind. Naturally I did not want to disappoint him, but I had to tell him that my heart was set on playing football. When he saw my mind was made up, he gave me all the support I needed.

I can't stress enough, however, that cricket was always very much my second sporting love – and still is. Dad and Everton Weekes went to school together and came from the same neighbourhood around Bridgetown. And he wasn't the only legend I came into contact with courtesy of my father. I remember the thrill of once meeting Clive Lloyd and Lance Gibbs, and I have to admit I have always supported the West Indies over England, even though we regularly had English teams coming on tour. I can't say for sure whether the rest of the islanders felt the same way as me. I guess it was probably pretty mixed in the sense that some felt their ties were to the Windies because of heritage and culture and others showed allegiance to England. I have one particular friend who will come after you if you say anything bad about England! But don't get me wrong, I admired the English players enormously. If the West Indies were not playing, I'd always root for England. I even played myself against the likes of Ray Illingworth and Fred Titmus, two of England's greatest spinners. If I'd opted for cricket, who knows, I might have become the new Gary Sobers and ended up as an all-rounder rather than a goal scorer.

I played against Sobers on one occasion. Like many West Indians, the great man played county cricket in England, in his case with Nottinghamshire. But the game in question was a Middlesex Select XI that included Sobers, Ken Barrington and Ray Illingworth. It was around the mid-60s and though I can't remember the score, what I do know is that, at just fifteen, I was in awe of the guy. So much so that I even had the same style of boot.

In those days the Windies were a huge force. Sometimes they just had to turn up in order for their big-name batters, bowlers and fielders to strike fear into the opposition with their strength, power and talent. They had such style and charisma that they were the team everyone wanted to beat. I worshipped many of the players back then though, if truth be told, the mid-1980s was probably their greatest era, peaking perhaps on their tour of England in 1984 where they won the series 5–0, the first time in Test cricket history the home team had been white-washed in a five-test series – or 'blackwashed' as it was humorously referred to. This was followed by a second clean sweep against England at home in 1985–86 as the Windies established the then-record of eleven consecutive Test victories. But sport is cyclical. For some reason they are lagging behind today, in Test cricket at least; they have a lot of talent, it's just a question of harnessing it correctly. Every team has a downturn – even Australia have had bad patches at one time or another. India at one time were the whipping boys, but now sides struggle to beat them. Right now, the game is probably more evenly matched than it's ever been and

England are right up there with the best.

Cricket has become far more of a global sport than when I was growing up, not just in terms of the numbers of countries who now play but the different formats. I know some people feel Twenty-20 and the 50-over game damages the sport but, for sheer excitement, I'm all in favour. You can have two games in a day and still get home at a reasonable time. The 2016 T20 World Cup in India was real edge-of-the-seat stuff. Naturally I was rooting for the West Indies in that dramatic final against England in Kolkata when Carlos Brathwaite took the game away from England in the last over with those four sixes. Poor Ben Stokes. He looked utterly distraught. I felt for him. Having said that, Test cricket is still the pinnacle, that's where you have to work for your runs and wickets.

PEOPLE ASK ME ALL THE TIME WHAT I WOULD HAVE BECOME IF I hadn't been a sportsman. The answer may surprise you: quite possibly a panel-beater. That's actually what I started out doing when I was about fourteen. We had a day release from school where once a week you'd do some kind of trade. Most of us leaned towards the kind of thing we thought we might go into when we left school in order to get early experience. I loved nothing more than to be able to see a car all messed up and make it look brand new again. Going to an all-boys school, you had to pick a trade of some description, so I picked panel-beating. But in truth, it was always sport for me. I could always look after myself physically – as opponents when I got to West Ham quickly discovered! But there was another reason why I don't think panel-beating would quite have worked me: there was just far too much banging! I can't stand too much noise and it was the same back then. It used to give me a headache. Thank goodness for football!

BY THIS TIME MY FATHER WAS WORKING IN THE PRISON SERVICE and our family moved into housing provided specially for us. Suddenly a whole new chapter in my life was beginning. In the dockyard was a massive building called the Casemates, a towering structure that used to house shells, ammunition, torpedoes and weapons for all the Royal Navy ships that visited Bermuda, as well as those stationed here as part of the West Indies Squadron. With the reduction in size of the Royal Navy after the Second World War, the building was no longer needed and was handed over to the Bermuda government to use as the main prison.

The dockyard itself became less important to the Royal Navy and many of its buildings were closed. Our house was right outside and the whole area became a huge adventure playground for the children who lived nearby. We played in and around all the stone buildings, dozens of which were padlocked. We even formed our own junior football team called Ireland Rangers (the dockyard part of Bermuda is called Ireland Island).

Our coach was the intriguingly named Ed 'Ice Water' Smith, assisted by Earl Glasgow and Hubby Rogers. Before you ask me why he was nicknamed Ice Water, I have to say I really don't know. All I can tell you is that he got the nickname from his father. Almost everyone had a nickname in Bermuda – and still does. Ed's brother was called Little Ice and he was called Big Ice. There you go. Even I was given a nickname, which I have to admit has stuck to me like glue ever since I was a kid. One of our best-known radio presenters, Joe Brown, was reading out the names of the teams when I was playing locally and for some reason called me Clyde 'Bunny' Best. Ever since, I've been known as Bunny – but only in Bermuda! Certainly no one at West Ham called me that. I made sure I kept it a Bermuda thing.

Ice Water Smith was a real disciplinarian, a no-nonsense kind of guy. I remember he would repeatedly warn us never to be late for training. I had to learn the hard way. One weekend we had to report early to our home field, called Moresby Plain, which I could actually see from my parents' bedroom window. Even being so close, for some reason I arrived late and 'Ice Water' left me out of the team to play that day. I ran home crying like a baby. The incident taught me a lesson, however, and from that day on, from schools football all the way through my professional career, I was never, ever late. Not once.

Our first year in the league was difficult. As a youth player, you could be any age between twelve and eighteen and we invariably found ourselves playing against boys who were four or five years older than us. However, we held together and worked hard as a unit, with my brother Carlton playing centre-half. Some people still say that Carlton was actually a better player than his younger brother. They don't know what they are talking about! I respected my brother hugely, but a better player than me? No way. He certainly had talent but simply didn't have the passion. Plus, he never really wanted to play at the top level. His was a different path, moving from accountancy to teaching. Good for him. Each to his own. He was a very quiet guy but in his own way he made just as great a contribution to Bermudian society as I did. I loved the way he was able to get through to the children. I think it's important that young children, especially males, have male teachers at some point in their schooling.

Carlton has always told me he is a West Ham fan, but deep down I think he had a sneaking leaning towards Arsenal. I forgave him for that! I was proud of the fact that he chose an education. If I could turn the clock back to my own school days, I'd probably have sat right at the front near the teacher. Although I always knew I wanted to play sport, I should probably have paid more attention in class. Education can get you a long way and I maybe should have been a bit more dedicated in case my football career didn't work out.

During my time with Ireland Rangers we would eagerly await the arrival of Royal Navy warships, such as the frigates HMS *Londonderry* and HMS *Plymouth*, the submarine HMS *Ocelot*, the destroyers HMS *Defender* and *Dainty* and some Royal Fleet Auxiliary ships, many of which were part of the West Indies Squadron.

Their crews were young and fit – and always looking for a game of football. Some of the sailors on those ships had represented the Royal Navy against the British Army and Royal Air Force. Our Ireland Rangers team played regularly against them, which meant I was a twelve-year-old playing against men twice my age. The sailors were tough defenders and skilful attackers – but even though I was conspicuous by my age I enjoyed every minute of those encounters. I learned how to keep possession of the ball, when to pass, how to get on the end of a cross, how to hold the ball up until the other strikers were in position. I will always be grateful to them for giving me part of my football education, even though I came home at night with my legs a mass of bruises. As I say, I was playing against much older and more experienced footballers, fully developed adults – yet I was holding my own. It really helped my development and made a big difference in later life.

Perhaps my size also had something to do with people getting the wrong impression about my age when I got to England. I've heard all kinds of stories about people saying I was actually older, but the fact is I was just big for my age, which I'd never lie about. God just gave me a good build. If I'd been a little pipsqueak, I'd probably have got knocked around, so I'm grateful for the physical attributes I had. People used to think twice about picking on me.

Let me put to bed another ridiculous myth, about me being born in the USSR. I really have no idea where that came from. I actually only recently heard about it, but it's a nonsensical and bizarre rumour that has no grounding in reality. Some people just pick something up and keep it in their minds, but it's complete nonsense. Black and born in Russia? I don't think so. In fact, I've never even been to eastern Europe. West Ham once played Dinamo Tbilisi in the old European Cup Winners' Cup but by then I was in the United States.

The Royal Naval Dockyard is now a tourist attraction, where gigantic cruise ships from the USA berth when they visit the island. The old Royal Navy buildings are shopping malls, restaurants and craft stores, but the area will forever be for me the place where my football skills were sharpened and honed.

✳

SUNSETS IN BERMUDA ARE SPECTACULAR. OUR TOURISTS HIRE small motorcycles and mopeds to drive through country lanes to our golf courses and beaches. The golden rays of the setting sun dance on the blue sparkling waters of the Atlantic Ocean and caress the pink sand on our beaches (yes, the sand is actually pink).

As the tourists settled down on their hotel verandas each evening for cocktails, and while Bermuda families prepared evening meals, I'd be on the football pitch at the dockyard with yet more pals – Charles Fubler, Stuart Wilkinson, Clyde Goines, Greg Rogers, Ed Bailey, Kent Dill, Alan Dill, Jerry Phillips, Mervin Smith, George Brangman, Cal Basden, Sheldon Bradshaw and, of course, my brother Carlton – passing, trapping, meeting corners from the left, from the right, shooting with both feet, working to perfect my skills. I wasn't even a teenager yet but I wanted to be like my name – the BEST!

After two years at Ireland Rangers, I moved on to Somerset, a much bigger club that had both a youth and a senior squad and where I'd seen my three cousins, Charles, Rudy and Lionel, playing; I wanted to emulate them. Charles was a terrific centre-half, Rudy was a midfielder who never stopped running and Lionel was a tall, rangy forward, who was superb in the air and was equally good with both feet. He could play in midfield or up front and he once scored 75 goals in a season. Regardless of the general standard of play in Bermuda, he was something special. Believe me, this guy could play. Tottenham Hotspur were interested in Lionel at one point and I'm convinced he could have made the grade, given the opportunity. Spurs came over one year on tour and beat a Bermuda Football Association XI 3–2. If I'm not mistaken, Lionel scored both the BFA goals and Bill Nicholson liked the look of him. Unfortunately, it didn't pan out. In those days, a lot of our boys – remember they were strictly amateur – were committed to their work and Lionel didn't fancy leaving his job as a plumber to take a chance on being a professional footballer.

When I got to Somerset, I started out with the youth team and no one could beat us. Our coach, Conrad Symonds, just let us play. Sadly, Conrad passed away in 2015. One thing about him was he never confused people. He told you your job, and you knew what you had to do, and he expected you to go and do it. That's how we functioned. He was a great person for football in Bermuda and I wish we had more people like him today because he did not mess around.

Conrad had done some work at Portsmouth before coming back home to take us over. Trophies galore came our way and that's when they started to call Somerset 'Silver City'. It wasn't long before I was in the senior side at around fourteen or fifteen. Conrad, who had seen me at youth level, decided it was time to elevate me for this particular game. I guess it all took off from there. When the best team in Jamaica, Santos, came to Bermuda on tour around Christmas, I got my chance. They were supposed to be coming here to teach us a football lesson but, as it turned out, we were the ones who did the teaching. We gave them a pasting, even though the score was tight at 3–2, with yours truly coming on as sub and netting one of them with a header from a left-wing cross. We were worthy winners and from that day, Conrad kept me in the team.

Conrad never took a coaching course – he didn't believe in badges – but he was an excellent mentor. While he was in England, he married an English girl and even after coming home continued to make trips to the UK to take a look at what the professional clubs were doing there. Then he'd be back in Bermuda again to impart some of that knowledge to us. We would work hard to improve. At Somerset we would often train four nights a week – Tuesday, Wednesday, Thursday and Friday. I was still at school and they were full days. But even then I knew that if I wanted to get to the top I would have to make sacrifices.

Once I had got into the Somerset first team I didn't find goals hard to come by. I never kept a count of how many I scored, but I remember I used to get them in fours and fives. One day we played Young Men's Social Club, who were top of the league. The ground at the Pembroke Hamilton Club was packed and they were shooting their mouths off about what they were going to do to us. We annihilated them 8–1 and I scored four. The best of the bunch was one I slotted home after a long dribble, prompting a mini pitch invasion.

We had two natural wingers, Bernard Brangman and Reggie Tucker, who could pass the ball as well as anybody. These guys worked together with an almost telepathic understanding. They could pick you out at any time – they were that good. Reggie was so quick he'd beat you in a flash. Bernard was slower, but he was accurate with his crosses and once he'd got past the full-back the opposition knew they were in trouble.

I remember us playing a semi-pro team from New York one night. We walloped them 5–1 and were doing things we didn't even realise we were capable of. It was great football, one-twos all over the park and great running off the ball. We had so many gifted athletes that it seemed easy to play to that standard.

That year, 1968, Somerset won the Bermuda FA Cup for the first time, beating Devonshire Colts 3–2 at BAA Field on 20 April. There must have been 4,000 people there. That may not seem too many compared with England but when you consider the population of Bermuda, which at that time stood at under 65,000, that's a pretty healthy attendance. Whole families used to come and we'd have coachloads of supporters.

I was delighted to have scored twice, not least because we owed Colts one for what they'd done to us the week before at our own ground when they had given us a 6–2 hammering in the league, our only defeat of the entire campaign. For some reason, Somerset always had a problem when we wore white – it seemed to put a hex on us – and we had worn white that day.

Jimmy Parsons, who played in midfield for Colts, was fantastic in the league game. Jimmy loved to run at people and, when he started on a weaving dribble, he was difficult to stop. He had been a team-mate of mine at Churchill school.

Conrad made five changes to the team for the cup final and threw in some youth players. We were vastly improved and I particularly remember one of the two goals I scored that day. I controlled a long ball on my chest outside the penalty area and before it hit the ground it was in the back of the net. Oliver Caisey was in goal for Colts and I was later told he was actually afraid of the ferocity of the shot when he saw it heading his way. That made it 2–2 after ninety minutes and two minutes into extra time, I turned and belted in the winner from fifteen yards.

Three weeks later, we played the Colts again in the Friendship Trophy final, a third meeting in succession. We won 2–1 and I got both goals. The league championship trophy and the FA Cup were already in the trophy cabinet, so now we had clinched the triple crown. That was history written. We had won everything. I only had one year with Somerset, but it was a glorious year.

The key to our success was that we were fit and we'd put in the time. The season started in September in those days and we'd be out training on 1 August. From what I see nowadays, kids in Bermuda don't have that sort of dedication. I think the players of today expect the coaches to do too much for them. Coaches can only do so much; in the end you've got to put in the work for yourself.

At that time, football was on a real high in Bermuda and I believe the level of talent was so great that most of the players in that Somerset team, given the opportunity, could easily have made the grade as professionals. We had people like Randy Horton, Richard Simmons, Roger Hunt, Larry Hunt, Bernard Brangman and Reggie Tucker. Again, they may seem to many readers like a list of anonymous names, but to my mind they were good enough to have followed me to England. Sometimes it's a lot to do with luck.

Randy actually went to school in England and attracted a lot of attention from Leeds United, but things did not quite work out, though he did enjoy a fine career in the North American Soccer League, playing for New York Cosmos, among others. He was big, strong, unbelievable in the air, and it was tough to get the ball off him. Randy and I played up front for Somerset and our opponents could not handle us. The pair of us were so strong in the air that they used to say when Somerset won a corner, it was as good as a penalty. Randy eventually went into politics and became Bermuda's Speaker of the House of Assembly. I'm not really a politically minded guy, and I try to keep away from it, but hats off to Randy, he's done well for himself. I was honoured to have played with him; we even lined up together once for the national team.

The good players were not all limited to Somerset. Every team was competitive. The Lewis brothers, Leroy and Eversley, both had trials in England, Leroy with Fulham, Eversley with Manchester United and Crystal Palace before signing for Aberdeen north of the border in 1961. He was a big inspiration for me. That bit older, he proved a Bermudian could make it overseas.

Junior Mallory was another who also played professionally in the English league with Cardiff City, but unfortunately his career was curtailed by injury, including cartilage trouble in both knees. Before all of them came defender Arnold Woollard, the first Bermudian to play in the English First Division, making ten top-flight appearances for Newcastle in the 1950s.

Arnold was a trailblazer. It was unheard of for a Bermudian to play overseas, let alone sign professional forms. Yet long before footballers were feted like pop stars, Arnold was heaving his leather boots, to great effect, over some of the most illustrious soccer pitches in England. I may be the best-known Bermudian to play overseas, followed perhaps by Shaun Goater, but Arnold was perhaps the best defensive player we have ever produced. What's more, he had the good fortune to play in the same team as Jackie Milburn and Frank Brennan against the likes of Danny Blanchflower, Johnny Haynes, Jimmy Hill and Billy Wright. The reason so little is known about him stems from the fact that his playing career ended almost four decades ago and that defensive players do not grab the headlines the way goal scorers like me do. As an eighteen-year-old, Arnold impressed the director of Northampton Town, Phillip Hutton, who was visiting Bermuda in 1949. At that time, Northampton were in Third Division South and Arnold soon found himself on a boat headed for England. When he stepped on the pitch for Northampton Town in August 1949, he became Bermuda's first professional player. Respect!

Arnold's first year with the Cobblers saw the club make it to the fifth round of the FA Cup and the following season they reached the fourth round, where they fell to Arsenal 3–2 before 72,408 fans at Highbury. After a three-year spell with Northampton, he moved on to the Midland League's Peterborough United, but he would soon be packing his bags again – this time to Newcastle, for £5,000, in December 1952.

Newcastle had arguably one of the strongest sides in England at the time. They won the FA Cup in 1951 and 1952 and lifted the trophy again in 1955 with a 3–1 victory over Manchester City. Arnold's debut took a while but it finally came in an away clash against Portsmouth on 18 April 1953. Even though he only played a handful of games for Newcastle before being sold to Bournemouth for £2,000, once he got to the south coast he took part in another great FA Cup giant-killing run.

Bournemouth were another Third Division South club, but in 1956/57 Arnold was part of the side that took care of Burton Albion, Swindon and Accrington then posting two huge upsets by beating the mighty Wolverhampton Wanderers 1–0 and then Tottenham Hotspur, before succumbing to Manchester United in the quarter-final. Arnold ended his professional career back where it had started at Northampton Town before returning to Bermuda, where he carried on playing before hanging up his boots for good in 1967 and going back to live in England.

Most of our young players nowadays will never have heard of people like Arnold. It is a serious weakness of Bermuda that we don't embrace our sporting history. We may not have international household names, but every country has its sporting heroes and we haven't done enough to preserve the sporting legacy of some of ours. Memories of great players are simply allowed to die. That's one reason why I believe football in Bermuda has declined so much, because the kids simply don't have role models from the past. We do at least have a Sports Hall of Fame, which the government opened just over a decade ago. But it's not really enough. Reverence for football history was one of the many things I appreciated about England. I mean, people still talk about the late Sir Stanley Matthews today.

WHO WERE THE OTHER BERMUDIANS TO MAKE THE GRADE IN England? Well, we had Shaun Goater, as previously mentioned, who used to poach goals for fun for Manchester City across three divisions. At the age of seventeen, Shaun left home to further his education in the United States, where he had received a soccer scholarship. While home in Bermuda during Thanksgiving one year he was spotted by scouts from Manchester United, who invited him to England for a trial. With encouragement from his mother, who was a former football player herself, he accepted, forfeiting his scholarship in the process.

Ironically it was at Manchester City where Shaun, who also had spells with Rotherham, Bristol City and Reading among others, made his name. 'Feed the Goat and he will score' was the chant, never more apt than during the 1998/99 season when he bagged 21, including the winner in a play-off semi-final against Wigan that sent City to Wembley for a play-off final that saw them promoted after a penalty shootout. The following season was even more prolific as the Goat was the club's top goal scorer once again, this time with 29 goals, and he was named Manchester City's Player of the Year. That summer he was awarded the freedom of Bermuda, with 21 June declared as 'Shaun Goater Day' on the island just for that one year.

Another notable Bermudian who went to ply his trade overseas was Kyle Lightbourne who, to paraphrase a famous saying, had more clubs than Jack Nicklaus. Kyle turned out for Scarborough, Walsall, Coventry City, Fulham, Stoke City, Swindon Town, Cardiff City, Macclesfield Town and Hull City, and won forty caps for his country.

You have to remember that all of these guys, just like me, were amateurs when they started out; it used to amaze people who visited us that a country so small could produce the number of quality players that we did.

Even after I'd left for England, I used to enjoy coming home either to play or help out in any way I was wanted. That was my way of giving back to my community. When I decided to take up football, my father always told me that I wasn't doing it for myself, that I was doing it for all the bus drivers, train drivers and hospital workers back home who were following my exploits, and to never allow it to go to my head. At the time I had a lot of friends in the hotel industry and if they were happy, so was I. Besides, Bermuda has always had a large diaspora outside the country, mostly in England – and I was doing it for them too. I tried never to forget where I came from – even though there are some footballers today who clearly don't have the same attitude.

3

LUCKILY NO ONE WAS KILLED

BEFORE I EVER KICKED A BALL IN ENGLISH FOOTBALL I WAS AL-ready an experienced international footballer. I started playing for Bermuda at the age of fifteen and enjoyed some amazing experiences in the World Cup, the Olympic qualifiers and the Pan American Games.

That international exposure was invaluable to me as a developing player. Since Bermuda had a population the size of a small town in England, the domestic competition was obviously limited. The other thing international football gave me was the chance to show off my abilities outside my own isolated country. Had I never played for Bermuda in my mid-teens, the chance to go to England might never have materialised. We have never qualified for the World Cup finals and have won only 13 of our 32 qualifiers over the years. In fact, the first time we even entered was for the 1970 tournament. But it was important for me to make some kind of mark on the international scene.

Our national squad in the late 1960s had remarkable team spirit. Though we were all from different parts of the island, fierce local rivalry was set aside and we were like one big, happy family. We had an English coach, Graham Adams, who worked us hard in training and was a fantastic motivator. Never mind that we were amateurs, our attitude to training was professional. When sessions were scheduled for 6 p.m., the players were there for 5.30 p.m. The reason we got there early was because you knew that if you messed up, someone else would be there to take your spot.

We showed what we were made of at the Pan American Games, the world's third largest international sporting festival, in Winnipeg, Canada, in the summer of 1967. Not only were we the smallest country ever to have competed in the competition, but this was Bermuda's first appearance in an international football tournament. We stunned everybody by reaching the final.

In the gold medal match we played mighty Mexico. No one gave us a prayer, but we came within a coat of paint of winning it. With the game goalless and just two minutes left, I leaped for a header and beat the goalkeeper, but it came back off the post. That's how close we came to a sporting miracle.

We had worked so hard to keep the Mexicans at bay over the ninety minutes that we were exhausted, and so crumbled in extra time, losing 4–0. However, we were proud of what we had achieved. The first Bermuda team to win a Pan American Games medal. In any sport. What a feeling! In those days, we could compete with countries like Mexico and the USA. I believe that even the USA team of today would have had their hands full if they had come up against that particular Bermuda side.

In fact, our first match in Section B in Winnipeg had been against the USA and we won 7–3. I didn't play in that game, nor the next group match, a 1–1 draw with Cuba. Maybe Adams didn't want to throw me into the lions' den because of my age and inexperience but I was never going to be so impertinent as to ask why. I was just pleased to be in the squad. Perhaps he had a rethink about whether I could handle the occasion, because he put me into the crunch match against host nation Canada in front of a sell-out 22,000 crowd, also in Winnipeg. We knew we had to get a result to advance and when we made a couple of bad defensive errors and went 2–0 down in the first fifteen minutes, our chances didn't look good. But we always believed in ourselves and came back strongly. Carlton (Pepe) Dill scored a goal in each half to give us a well-deserved draw. I had a decent enough game and created both goals.

The point we earned was enough to put us through to the semi-finals, where we played Trinidad & Tobago. Dill gave us a 1–0 half-time lead, then Gary Darrell put us two up before Trinidad pulled one back midway through the second half. Three minutes later, Dill played the ball through to me and I brought it down and just whacked it in from the edge of the penalty area. That sealed our 3–1 win and guaranteed a medal for us regardless of what happened in the final.

There was jubilation back in Bermuda when we returned with our silver medals. As soon as we got home, immaculately dressed in our Bermuda shorts and blazers, we were met at the airport by dignitaries and a fifty-car motorcade took us to the City Hall in Hamilton, where thousands turned out to cheer us. It was an exciting, proud and emotional moment for me. I was still a teenager.

There was a lot of creative ability in that team and we considered ourselves entertainers. People were keen to watch us. I remember an Olympic qualifier against Guatemala at the National Stadium in December 1967 which drew a crowd of more than 8,000. I believe it was the biggest crowd Bermuda has ever seen for a sporting event, about one-seventh of our population at that time.

We had caught the imagination of the country by eliminating the USA from the Olympic qualifiers earlier that year. After drawing 1–1 at home, we won the second leg 1–0 at Comiskey Park in Chicago, thanks to Gladwyn Daniels' winner. We followed that up with our Pan American silver medal and interest in the national team was at an all-time high.

We had already drawn 1–1 in Guatemala and needed to win the home leg to qualify for the following year's Olympic Games in Mexico City. We did everything but score in a match that ended goalless after ninety minutes. Bizarrely, the referee abandoned the still-scoreless game seventeen minutes into extra time, because it had become too dark to play. We had no floodlights back then.

The Guatemalans were quite prone to play-acting – in my experience, often a hazard of playing against Latin American teams. Afterwards the visitors claimed they had been 'afraid of the crowd', since in their own country the fans watched from behind fences, whereas there were no barriers in Bermuda. Afraid of a Bermuda crowd? Per-lease! . . . OK, there had been one flashpoint when a Bermuda fan had run onto the field and pushed two Guatemalan players as they tried to carry a cramp-stricken team-mate off the pitch. But the accusations against us were way over the top, the visitors even claiming that the president of the Guatemalan Olympic Association had been punched in the face – which turned out to be complete nonsense.

All of this added spice to the replay of the abandoned game, which FIFA decided for some unknown reason to stage in El Salvador rather than let us host it again. You'd have to ask FIFA why they took that decision but we Bermudians are pretty laid-back people and we went along with it. What we encountered on the field, however, still makes me come out in a cold sweat to this day.

The National Stadium in San Salvador was supposed to be a 'neutral venue' – but as El Salvador and Guatemala are neighbouring countries, it really was like an away match for us. The Guatemalan fans poured over the border, packed the stadium and created an intimidating atmosphere. To get some idea of how passionate about football the region was, it is perhaps worth recalling at this juncture that roughly a year after our visit, El Salvador and another of its neighbours, Honduras, actually took up arms over a football match. In what became known as the Soccer War, ostensibly over which of the two would qualify for the 1970 World Cup in Mexico, the fighting only lasted 100 hours but thousands lost their lives and thousands more were rendered homeless.

Luckily no one was killed when we took on Guatemala, though it was on a par with the acid incident described at the start of this book as the scariest time I can recall in my career. We concentrated on our task and took a first-half lead with a goal by Rudy Smith. The crowd was becoming increasingly frustrated as we held on to that scoreline until late in the game. It was apparent that they were not about to take defeat well and the fear that they would invade the pitch and physically harm us was very real. In his half-time team talk, coach Adams suggested we should run to the centre circle if any thugs charged on at the end and rely on the armed Salvadorean police to protect us.

As the minutes ticked by, the fans edged progressively closer to the touchline. It was clear there was going to be trouble. So it proved. In the 89th minute, our defence finally cracked and Guatemala equalised. Pandemonium broke out. Thousands ran onto the field and hurled bottles and cans at us, even though their team had just levelled. I guess, being mad about football, they probably thought they should have beaten us, Bermuda being such a small country. The police had guns, but that did not deter the idiots. Some of the fans even set fire to the stadium and we were herded into the centre circle to get as far away from the flames as we could. The authorities brought it under control but, needless to say, it was a terrifying situation; it would have been far worse if we had held on to win. As the gaffer said afterwards: 'If we had won, we would have been dead men. I doubt whether many of us would have survived.' Adams himself had been punched twice in the stomach, once with a knuckleduster, as he tried to restrain the marauding yobs.

It took twenty minutes for the pitch to be cleared so we could restart the match. There were no flags to mark the halfway line but that was the least of our worries. It was a testament to our strength of character that we managed to compose ourselves and press forward, looking for victory in extra time, in spite of the obvious concerns about what could happen to us.

I cracked in a shot that the Guatemalan goalkeeper managed to tip away and Daniels also went close, before Guatemala grabbed the winner. We had lost the match – but thankfully not our lives – and our Olympic dream had come to a violent end. I have never seen anything like it since on a football field, and hopefully never will again.

4

NOT THE 'BEST' OF STARTS

TO THIS DAY CLARET AND BLUE BLOOD RUNS THROUGH ME, BUT let me explain how the affinity with West Ham started. Most kids in Bermuda supported Manchester United or Liverpool and I initially had a soft spot for Tottenham, which I'll explain shortly. You have to go back to the Hammers' 1964 FA Cup final against Preston to understand how my allegiance changed and when the West Ham love affair began. I was watching the game with my brother on television and as an impressionable youngster was so enthralled, I turned to him and said, 'One day I'm going to play for that team.'

I know it sounds a ridiculously unlikely prophecy but I promise you it's true. The cup final in those days, you see, meant everything to anyone who was nuts about the game. It was one of the very few live televised matches we ever got back home. Kids tends to support the team winning things at the time they are growing up and I was no different, hence the fact that my preferred team before that was Tottenham. Whisper that ever so softly to West Ham fans, but I'm afraid it's the truth.

I'd seen Spurs in the 1963 Cup Winners' Cup final against Atletico Madrid and it had a profound effect on me. It was probably the first time I decided I wanted to be a professional footballer so it was no surprise that I followed Spurs for a short while. Then I switched to Manchester United (as people did and still do!) but I became strictly a Hammer from the 1964 FA Cup final onwards. Yet you know what? I'd actually forgotten about watching the game with my brother

Carlton until he reminded me many years later, which brought it all back. Back in June 2014, my club in Somerset honoured me with a banquet and it actually brought tears to my eyes when Carlton stood up to make a speech and reminded everyone about how starstruck I had been all those years ago.

It was no surprise that when the 1966 World Cup came round, I was enthralled by the West Ham connection. I remember watching the final at Wembley on television with one of my best friends. He pretended to be Martin Peters and I was Geoff Hurst. All it did was serve to fuel my ambition to join the Hammers, but I could scarcely imagine that a couple of years later I'd actually be playing with these guys in the flesh. And all courtesy of Graham Adams, the guy who had been coaching me at national-team level. Boy, what a debt I owe Graham, who knew Ron Greenwood and arranged a trial for me.

*

THAT NIGHT IN AUGUST 1968 AS THE PLANE TOOK OFF INTO THE INK-black sky heading northeast to England will always be etched in my memory. I watched as the pretty white roofs below faded from view and the Boeing 707 started climbing to 30,000 feet. As the cabin crew moved round, preparing supper, I had time to sit back and reflect on my last night at home. We all got together as a neighbourhood and everyone wished me well. Leaving Bermuda at the age of seventeen was virtually unheard of, let alone flying across to Europe. I knew I was going to a colder climate so it was important I packed warm clothing. I was leaving nothing to chance and did quite a lot of the packing myself – having been in the boy scouts, you learn that sort of thing! I'd never been to Europe but a lot of my schoolteachers were from the UK and I'd chatted with a few of them in terms of what to expect.

I also reflected on what an amazing season it had been playing for Somerset, who had become known as the Trojans. There have been lots of 'deadly strike forces' in modern football – Puskas and Di Stefano for Real Madrid, Denis Law and Bobby Charlton for Manchester United, Ian Rush and Kenny Dalglish for Liverpool. And this past season in Bermuda there had been another deadly duo – Randy Horton and Clyde Best. In the end, our partnership helped our club win everything in sight.

After supper was served on the flight, the lights were dimmed in the cabin and I began to reflect on our final game of that season – that BFU Friendship Trophy final in a packed ground in St George's. The Colts had torn right into us from the whistle and, to make matters more difficult, our centre-half Kenny Cann collided with a Colts' player during the first 45 minutes and did not reappear after the interval. It was a bad blow. Kenny was a marvellous pivot and had just been voted Bermuda's Most Valuable Player of the Year.

I wasn't having a great match. We were trailing 1–0 at half-time through a splendid goal by Colts' skipper Cal Simmons and neither Randy nor I were making much progress against their centre-backs. Our defence was constantly threatened by the skilful probing of their midfield. I remember one moment of panic when Gary Darrell swept the ball into our goalmouth and our goalie Clyde Burrows blocked Louis De Silva's attempt to score.

Gradually, though, we tightened our grip on the game. I started playing wide, leaving Randy to go it alone through the middle. Twenty minutes after half-time I pounced, forcing the ball home between Colts' goalie Oliver Caisey and the near post.

Soon afterwards I had the ball in the net again and fans spilled onto the field to celebrate, unaware that the offside flag had gone up. Four minutes from time I got on the end of a George Brangman corner and flicked the ball home for 2–0. Even though it finished 2–1, what a way it was to end the season.

I reflected on all of this during the seven-hour journey to the UK. I had no idea what life would be like in England. Neither did my family. They had all come to the airport to wish me bon voyage that beautiful Bermuda evening without really knowing what I was letting myself in for. I already knew quite a bit about London, having played against a lot of guys who had been in the Royal Navy, plus I'd been friends with quite a few people who had been there before, including a number of my schoolteachers. All of them had told me it was a fantastic city and that I would never get bored. Coming from an English colony, I was used to things like driving on the left, but I knew that getting accustomed to the harsh weather, compared to Bermuda at least, would be a tough challenge. Still, I was anxious to get there since I had set a goal for myself and that was to be a professional in England. As the cabin crew cleared up supper trays, I thought to myself: Somerset did not just defeat other sides in the Bermuda First Division.

They 'hammered' them. Hammer. The Hammers. West Ham.

A few months previously I had played hooky from school with some of my classmates to watch Manchester United win the European Cup against Benfica in May 1968. If someone had told a seventeen-year-old Clyde Best that within two years or so I would be playing against the likes of Denis Law, Bobby Charlton and, of course, the other 'Best' – George – I would have fallen off my seat laughing, and probably so would everyone else. But that is exactly what was to come. I gradually fell asleep during the flight, only waking up when we were over England's south coast. We were approaching Heathrow – and outside everything looked awfully grey.

I had a suitcase and hand luggage with me. After going through customs I looked around to see who had come to meet me. Would it be Mr Greenwood? Of course not, he was far too important. The club secretary, perhaps? Or maybe the youth-team coach? I waited and waited – it must have been for a good hour – before it dawned on me that I was on my own in this huge metropolis that was alien to me in every way and that no one was coming. I needed to get to the ground before it got dark so I lugged my bags onto the airport bus to take me to Victoria station. When people think of London they think of Big Ben, Buckingham Palace and Piccadilly Circus. All of those tourist attractions are in the West End, but West Ham is also part of London and isn't on the west side at all. It is very firmly in east London and proud of it, but I had no idea at the time about how long it would take to get from one part of London to the next. Not for the last time, I examined a tube map, thanked my lucky stars that Victoria, as well as being a main-line station, was also on the District Line and hoped for the best, watching intently as the train passed through underground stations that were just names on a map for me: Whitechapel, Stepney, Bow. I got off at the stop marked West Ham, assuming this was where the ground was. No one had told me anything different. Little did I know. All I could do was wander around until a kindly gentleman pointed out that Upton Park was actually some distance away.

I COULDN'T BELIEVE WHAT WAS HAPPENING TO ME. TO SAY IT was an inauspicious start is an understatement. Surely this wasn't the sign of things to come? It was a Sunday night and Heathrow airport had been teeming. I had never seen so many people in one place in my life. It could not have been a bigger contrast to back home and I instantly felt I had made the wrong decision. If I'd had a return plane ticket, in all honestly I would probably have flown straight home. I kid you not. I was that depressed. I was dumbfounded that there was no one to meet me. I thought clubs in England, like at home, operated on Sundays (which they do these days) and that someone was bound to turn up. Big mistake. My only option had been to somehow get across town. Thank goodness for the aforementioned stranger who started walking across the street towards me. He obviously could tell I was somewhat bewildered and asked me if he could help. I told him I was supposed to be coming for a trial at West Ham and that I couldn't find the club. His reply wasn't exactly what I wanted to hear: that the club had played the day before and was not open.

As I questioned what on earth I had let myself in for, the old man pointed towards the local park. 'One of the players' mother lives there,' he told me. 'I'll take you there.' Which is exactly what he did. When I knocked at the door of 23 Ronald Avenue, a certain Mrs Jessie Charles, mother of John and Clive, gave me a quizzical look and wondered who the heck this stranger was, knocking at her door out of the blue. She could have slammed it straight in my face. She was a small white lady and I was a bulky black teenager. For all she knew, I could have been there to rob the house. Yet we struck up an immediate affinity – even on the doorstep, I can't explain why. Maybe she thought I was some distant cousin, since one of her husbands had been from the Caribbean. When I explained the situation, however, she immediately took me in. It was an extraordinary act of generosity. I literally had no idea where else I would have stayed that night. I didn't know the area at all and it was getting dark. Conversely, she didn't know me from Adam yet welcomed me with open arms. I'm indebted to that family for so much – as I will mention time and time again. They played a key role in my upbringing. I ended up staying with Jessie, apart from a few months elsewhere, until I got married several years later. She was like a second mum to me. Even now, whenever I go back to England, I always make sure I see one of the family.

5

FIRST IMPRESSIONS

BRITISH FOOTBALL WAS IN ITS ASCENDANCY IN THE MID-TO-LATE 1960s. England were reigning World Champions. In May 1967 Glasgow Celtic became the first British team to win the European Cup, breaking the stranglehold that European clubs such as Inter Milan and Real Madrid had on the trophy. Players like Jimmy Johnstone and Billy McNeil were becoming household names all over Europe; and West Ham had also brought pride to the UK by winning the now defunct European Cup Winners' Cup in 1965, defeating 1860 Munich at Wembley 2–0.

The area around Upton Park is not like fashionable Belgravia or snobbish Westminster. West Ham is a working-class area where the main industry used to be shipbuilding, with massive workshops and dry docks and where the constant 'clanging of hammers' was heard. Mighty warships were built there.

The original club was called Thames Ironworks FC (hence the chant 'Come On You Irons') but it was wound up in 1900 and relaunched as West Ham United FC. The club emblem incorporated the crossed 'hammers' of the old Thames Ironworks emblem and introduced a castle in the background. I only discovered recently that Anne Boleyn, one of the wives of Henry VIII, had a castle in the area and that eventually the stadium was named the Boleyn Ground in her honour.

During the Second World War the whole of the East End of London was bombed relentlessly by the German Luftwaffe and many of the old terraced houses near the river were destroyed completely. The East Enders are a chirpy lot, however. When I arrived over twenty years after the war had finished, there seemed to be building going on all over the place, with new tower blocks replacing the houses obliterated by the bombing. Old-time East Enders to this day say that those tower blocks were a mistake and that much of the community spirit vanished when the high-rise flats were built. Still, there seemed to be a lot of the old East End there when I arrived that Sunday evening.

West Ham was never a rich London club like Spurs or Chelsea – they didn't have the funds to buy 'big name' players. Instead, they nurtured their own. After the war, they set about redeveloping the team. The manager at the time was Ted Fenton. A forward-thinking individual, he pushed for the establishment of an academy at West Ham to bring on and develop young players. He made some excellent signings, including Malcolm Allison, John Bond, Dave Sexton, Jimmy Andrews and Frank O'Farrell. Right across from the Boleyn Ground sat the Café Cassettari, where Ted Fenton made a deal with the owners to provide meals and drinks for players at a price the club could afford. Fenton would encourage the players to sit around the tables talking tactics, using cutlery and salt-and-pepper shakers to illustrate moves. The tradition carried on under Ron Greenwood and I have fond memories of long evenings there talking football, football and more football with the other West Ham players.

Four years before I arrived, Ron had guided West Ham to that famous FA Cup triumph over Preston North End I had watched on television with my brother, then the European Cup Winners' Cup trophy a year later. Greenwood's team was built around West Ham's three iconic England World Cup winners: skipper Bobby Moore in defence, Martin Peters in midfield and Geoff Hurst up front. They were all products of the successful youth set-up – which became known as the Academy of Football – founded by Fenton.

Bobby had made his debut for West Ham aged seventeen in 1958, four years before starting his illustrious England career. Incidentally, when he was signed as a Hammers apprentice in 1955, his wages were £7 . . . per month, that is. How times have changed.

When Sir Alf Ramsey was manager of England he famously described Martin Peters, after a game against Scotland, as the first 'modern midfielder' who was 'ten years ahead of his time', while Geoff Hurst was a natural striker and his goal-scoring record in the FA and League Cup stood for over thirty years until it was overtaken by Liverpool's Robbie Fowler. Geoff was originally a midfielder but Ron Greenwood converted him to a striker and it paid dividends both with West Ham and the national side.

In Bermuda, everyone knows everyone else – or so it seems a lot of the time. We know each other through school, church, workplace, football, golf and other sports clubs, and obviously through our extended families. Growing up in the 1950s and 60s seemed very uncomplicated to me. Everyone in Somerset Village knew that I was 'Joseph Best's *bye*' (that's how we say 'boy' in Bermuda). We did not need formal addresses for our postmen in those days. We just said, 'Oh, we live in Scaur Hill, it's a pink house with white blinds,' or, 'You turn into Scott's Hill Road and you will see a cedar tree in a large garden: that's our house – the water tank is at the left-hand side.'

As I said earlier, Bermuda has no natural fresh water for drinking and washing. We catch rainwater on our lime-washed roofs, after which it drains into a large tank either beneath or next to the house. From there it is pumped up into the house for showers, baths and washing. Bermudians are very careful when it comes to conserving water. We do not waste a drop because we never know when the next shower of rain is coming. Bermuda has about sixty inches of rain every year but sometimes we can go for weeks on end without a drop falling, and that's when we have to start purchasing water in 1,000-gallon loads from licensed water dealers.

Old habits die hard and I carried this frugality with me throughout my football career, whether in digs or hotels, using just enough water in the shower and turning it off immediately I was finished. I guess you could call it being somewhat OCD, but I felt it the right thing to do in terms of not wasting. I hate waste in any shape or form.

Although my first few days were spent at the home of Mrs Charles, West Ham had already found me alternative digs at the home of Ted and Dot Dexter and their son Philip at 53 Dongola Road in nearby Plaistow. I liked it there but I yearned to go back to the Charles' and, when the opportunity arose, I first moved into a little hotel on Green Street named the Greenwood Hotel until Mrs Charles had got everything ready. One day during training Clive told me he'd asked his mum if I could go and live with them permanently. When he got his answer, I didn't hesitate. It wasn't that I was unhappy, I just felt more comfortable being with someone I was spending time with. I'd been back to the Charles' house even when I was living with the Dexters, you see. Most afternoons, we'd go back to Clive's and play records on his turntable. The Four Tops, the Temptations, that kind of thing. Needless to say, it was a great feeling going back to the Charles family. They treated me like one of their own.

The evenings were lengthening and the days growing shorter. It seemed to rain a lot and the weather turned damp and cold as the children finished their summer holidays and returned to school. During this time, the teenage Clyde Best was introduced to an English gastronomic tradition: roast beef, Yorkshire pudding, Brussels sprouts and roast potatoes. It was a typical English diet which I grew to love, and helped to ward off the chilly winter that was fast approaching.

I also had to get used to all sorts of different street names – Romford Road, Green Street, Manor Park. I was overwhelmed by it all – the signs on bus stops showing different routes, underground stations with all those colours representing various lines. To say everything was all a culture shock is another understatement. To me, you see, it was second nature back home to say 'good morning' or 'good afternoon'. When I arrived in England and did the same thing to complete strangers, they'd look at me like I was totally crazy. But in Bermuda, if a greeting like that doesn't get a response, you can bet you're going to get told off. People would think there was something wrong with you. That's just the way we are. That's the way we are brought up. Mind you, when you wake up every morning and the sun's shining, it's hard not to be happy. It puts a smile on your face.

Having said that, being in the middle of the Atlantic Ocean, we are susceptible to more extremes of weather back home than in England. The worst storm in a decade occurred in October 2014, when Hurricane Gonzalo lashed Bermuda with winds of about 110mph. As far as I remember, about 80 per cent of the island lost power as the winds felled trees and damaged many of our buildings, including the main hospital. Luckily no one died, but it was a horrible reminder of how vulnerable we are to the natural elements.

FORTUNATELY I WAS NOT TOO FAR FROM UPTON PARK WHEN I lived with the Dexter family – I could walk to the ground in about fifteen minutes.

What a change from our tiny island in the Atlantic Ocean, where South Shore Road runs the whole length of Bermuda, meandering through our nine parishes until it gets to Somerset Village and then on to the dockyard.

I turned up for training at Chadwell Heath that first day after being collected in the van used for the apprentices, and reported to Albert Walker, the club's equipment manager. Quite a few of the other apprentices would become good friends of mine – John McDowell, Tony Carr, Terry Scales, Pat Holland, Steven Leigh, Peter Carey, Carl Humphrey, Keith Pointer and, more than any of them, Clive Charles, whose house I was to live in.

One of the first things I discovered was exactly why no one had turned up to meet me at Heathrow. It wasn't only that the club didn't work on a Sunday. They had apparently sent a telex requesting me to arrive on the Monday, but I never received it. Telecommunications back then were not that sophisticated. But at least I was where I should be and the sense of excitement was almost palpable. Not least when walking towards me were some of the most famous names in football. Within minutes of arriving, I was being introduced to Bobby Moore, Geoff Hurst and Martin Peters. Just imagine the effect that had on an impressionable seventeen-year-old. I could hardly control myself, but stayed silent and respectful. Geoff had scored three times in the World Cup final two years earlier and here I was having my photo taken with him. Not many people get that opportunity.

I had assumed that the first-team players went somewhere else for their training, and I could hardly take my eyes off them. The training ground at Chadwell Heath was about thirty minutes away in the direction of Romford. It was a journey I would get to know very well as time went on, but initially I would press my nose against the van window, taking in all the sights and sounds – the rows of terraced houses and tower blocks giving way to the suburbs: and all those greenhouses and little gardens full of potatoes, peas, cabbages and beetroot. All the houses seemed to have neat little vegetable gardens. I suppose it was a legacy from the war, when everyone had to 'Dig for Victory'.

Our youth-team coach was John Lyall, a future manager of West Ham. It was club policy to include the apprentices in every aspect of training – which meant that I was now working and learning from men who had won the World Cup. I and the other apprentices were included in the four-, five- and six-a-side games, plus the running and fitness exercises.

Within a week of arriving, I was playing competitive football, first in the Youth League then the Football Combination, made up of reserve teams, many of which contained first-team players who were coming back after injury.

We travelled all over the London area playing in these leagues. I have fond memories of the Lacey's bus company coming to pick us up at the Boleyn Ground and taking us to all kinds of places like Stevenage, Reading and even to play the London Metropolitan Police team.

After training each day at Chadwell Heath, we would return to Upton Park to shower and change – then go straight over to 'Mama Cass's' café with our vouchers for lunch and drinks. We used to go there at least twice a day. It became a regular haunt if you had anything to do with West Ham.

I kind of knew just two weeks into my trial that I had a good chance of being taken on. Ron Greenwood had privately told me as much. But for nine months or so, I had to prove myself in the youth and A teams. Work, work, work, improve, improve, improve. I just had to be patient.

6

INTERNATIONAL DUTY CALLS

SUDDENLY, AT THE END OF OCTOBER 1968, I WAS WINGING MY way home to Bermuda.

I remember seeing the coral reefs off St David's Head as the BOAC 707 swept low over the white roofs of the houses, touching down at the US Kindley Air Force Base. Home! The ground crew opened the door, brought the steps up and I could smell the fragrance of Bermuda once more and watch the waves dancing on the crystal-clear waters of Castle Harbour. Along with Carlton 'Peppy' Dill and Gladwin 'Bubba' Daniels, who were playing professionally overseas, I had been given permission by my club to help Bermuda prepare for a World Cup qualifier against the USA.

My family were waiting at arrivals, making a fuss of me, asking all about England and West Ham and all the big names of English football who I had met. I hardly had time to tell them. In fact, I had to prepare to fly out almost immediately with the Bermuda team to Kansas City, where we would play the USA. Canada were also in our section and although we drew 0–0 with them in Bermuda, they had thumped us 4–0 on their home turf.

I was really looking forward to representing my country again. Although we were rank outsiders, we still had a chance of making it to the 1970 World Cup finals. But the anticipation of taking on the Americans in Kansas gave way to huge disappointment as we were destroyed 6–2. We were not just beaten, we were taken apart, although the scoreline does not tell the whole story. We were drawing 2–2 after I equalised early in the second half, before we lost our goalkeeper, Granville ('The Cat') Nusum, in horrific circumstances. He collided with our skipper Kenny Cann and suffered a double fracture of the jaw. There were no substitute keepers in those days, so the injury cost us dear. The weird thing is that the Americans lost their goalkeeper, Sandy Feher, as well. He sustained a broken leg in the first five minutes. But their ten were far better than our ten.

We did not play well, we lost the meaning of defending, we were not co-ordinated. We could not get to grips with the Americans. They were just too strong and we returned to Bermuda crestfallen.

When I got home to the family and unpacked my bags properly, everyone wanted to hear not about the World Cup qualifier but about West Ham. 'Did you meet Bobby Moore?' I was constantly asked. Only two years previously the whole of Bermuda – and the rest of the world, it seemed – had watched Bobby lead England out against West Germany at Wembley. 'Meet him?' I would answer. 'I played six-a-side football with him the week I arrived in England!'

As temperatures in the UK plummeted and my West Ham team-mates played in rain, fog and mist in the Youth League and Football Combination, the club gave me permission to stay on at home and prepare for the Bermuda Youth International tournament, which was to take place over the Christmas holidays.

Six teams were involved: Bermuda, Barbados, Canada, Haiti, Mexico and USA. All of them had quality but we were confident we could lift the trophy.

Alan Richardson, who played for Pembroke Hamilton Club, was appointed as captain and yours truly became vice-captain. The teams were split into two groups. In Group A were Mexico, Canada and the USA while we were placed in the other group along with Haiti and Barbados.

All the teams stayed at Warwick Camp, which rapidly became an international village for the tournament. In our first game we steamrollered Barbados, smashing seven past them without reply. They simply could not match us. I hammered in three and Richard Simmons scored twice, with Mel Lewis and David Frost getting one apiece.

Next up came Haiti – what a thriller! We had 2,500 spectators at the National Stadium cheering us on. The game was tied 2–2 at half-time, and we were down 4–2 with ten minutes to go before Dale Russell and Calvin Raynor got us back on level terms.

In the end we tossed a coin to see who would top the group and Haiti won, which meant we would face Mexico in the semi-final. Sadly, it is a game I remember most of all for its lack of sportsmanship by the Mexicans. This was a youth tournament, remember – teenage players who were doing their best to represent their respective countries in the best spirit of the game. It wasn't some all-important senior World Cup qualifier.

Unfortunately Mexico seemed to forget what sportsmanship meant. They argued constantly with the referee, stole yardage at free kicks, and tried to kick the living daylights out of us. They even tried to pull the ball out of the hands of our goalie. After issuing warnings, referee Keith Dunstan eventually sent off their defender Ibarra.

It was all square after ninety minutes, then during extra time Roger Hunt – no relation to the great 1966 World Cup star – slipped the ball through to me and I made no mistake. Even down to ten men the Mexicans were still dangerous, however, and Jesus Preto took advantage of a mix-up in our defence to equalise. Their antics were still not over. The Mexican captain, already ejected from the game, was called back to flip the coin which would decide the eventual winner. He refused. When a team-mate did the honours instead, 'Tails!' I shouted – correctly. We were through to the final! I remember the crowd pouring onto the pitch and lifting us shoulder high as if we had already won the tournament.

We played the final against Haiti on New Year's Eve 1968, at the National Stadium. And what a game it was, just as the previous encounter with them had been. This time we smashed three past them without reply. They were never in the game. We outran and outplayed them from the first whistle. Over 4,000 fans turned up to cheer us on and we did not let them down.

Our first goal came from a corner kick. Mel Lewis chipped the ball to Roger Hunt, who flicked it on to me. I duly smashed it past the startled Haitian goalie, Joseph. Another goal arrived when Mel passed to Richard Simmons, who then slipped it to yours truly, and once again Joseph had to pick it out of the back of the net. A few minutes before half-time the game ended as a contest when Dale Russell lashed home a twenty-yarder that gave Joseph no chance. I was a mere seventeen, but from Dale's perspective I must have seemed like someone entering middle age. He was only fourteen.

At the end of the game the stadium erupted as His Excellency the Governor

Lord Martonmere presented us with the trophy – a handsome cedar football replica. Alan Richardson, our skipper, had been out injured for the game so I was stand-in captain and went up to receive it. Naturally, it was one of the proudest moments of what was then a fledgling career. I also ended up being top scorer for the tournament along with the Haitian centre-forward.

In late December in Bermuda, the light fades by 5 p.m. While the days can be warm, temperatures can drop into the low 50s or even high 40s Fahrenheit (around 10ºC) overnight. As I led the players off the field that night my thoughts were turning once more to a frozen football ground over 4,000 miles from this beautiful jewel in the Atlantic Ocean. It was tempting to stay on even longer, but I loved West Ham and on the evening of 2 January 1969, I once again boarded a BOAC flight from Bermuda to Heathrow.

7

PROUD HAMMER

I FELT MUCH MORE CONFIDENT THAN I HAD FIVE MONTHS PREVI-
ously. After all, I had captained a national side to victory. Even if it was only a
youth tournament, the pressures are, in their own way, just as great. As soon as
I was back at the Boleyn Ground I got stuck in with the rest of my mates in the
youth and reserve teams. But now I had to adapt to being back in a northern
hemisphere city slap-bang in the middle of winter. There was no proper daylight
until about 9 a.m. – and it was dark by mid-afternoon. Rain fell in torrents and
often became sleet. But training in these conditions was good for me. It tough-
ened me up (who says black players can't play in all conditions?) and prepared
me for the rest of my football career.

Not long after I got back, even though I still hadn't made my first-team
debut, I found myself unexpectedly lining up alongside three of West Ham's
top players. The first team was to play against Manchester City but the game
was postponed and the trio were asked if they would play in the reserves against
Northampton instead. The three were Bobby Moore, John Sissons and Ron
Boyce. We 2–1 but for much of the game my mind was in a blur.

A few days later, on 24 February, I turned eighteeen. It was a big birthday but
there was no partying. I had to train the following day so I wasn't prepared to
turn up for training worse for wear. In any case, I was not a heavy drinker, never
have been. I had one ambition and one ambition alone. To sign professional
terms and claw my way into the first team.

It didn't take much longer. On 14 March 1969, I took a massive step forward in my career. Ron Greenwood told me he wanted to see me up in the office and I knew instinctively it could only be one of two things. It was either welcome to the show, or sorry, we're letting you go. I tried not to show my nerves as I knocked on his door. He immediately put me at ease by saying he had some good news. I was being signed on a one-year deal. I guess they wanted a proper look at me and I understood that. If I did well for a year, I reasoned, they would take me on for longer. If truth be told, I wasn't that keen on a long-term deal anyway for fear of getting stuck in one place if things didn't work out. In those days, clubs had all the power. It was a far cry from the Bosman ruling, which didn't kick in until the mid-1990s and heralded the start of player power. Back then, if you signed a long-term contract, it was very difficult to break out of. Luckily, things worked very well indeed. All the young pros at the time were on the same pay, I think I started off on around forty pounds a week. Compared to the average person in the street that was a lot of money.

I couldn't wait to ring home. We had a phone at the Charles' but I always used to pay her when I called my family. In those days it was far more expensive than it is now, and you had to go through an operator, but I always managed to get through.

It has to go down as one of the most exciting days of my life but, taking my father's advice, I refused to let it go to my head and never stopped training, working at my game. I may have my faults but being big-headed was never one of them. Bobby Moore played a big part in that. He always tried to behave properly, on and off the pitch. And look what he managed to achieve. Why should I have been any different? Big-headed players at some point have to come down off their high horse, because one day your career is going to be all over and you still have to function in society.

I just don't think it's right being arrogant and disrespectful to people and it seems to have paid off, because I still get fan mail. I recently received a letter from Poland asking for a signed photo. Fans often stop by my house if they are visiting Bermuda. Most recently I had a group of Spurs fans show up; they were on vacation and their tour operator told them where I was living. I didn't feel in the least put out, and usually I'm happy to oblige. I grew up being respectful to people and hopefully I have lost none of that.

Some of it has to do with my Christian faith. A lot of my mother's family were involved with the Salvation Army so I used to go to church quite a bit when we were younger – though in truth I had little choice. I wouldn't necessarily say I was religious but I do believe in God – there's a difference – and I certainly feel I'm a spiritual person and have at times used my faith to deal with various setbacks. Sometimes I agreed to disagree with my parents about church, but I still had to go with the flow – a common trait in Bermuda. Having said that, I've always believed there is someone up there higher than me and I never take anything for granted. I'm a Christian but I keep my spirituality inside and don't go around shouting my mouth off about it. We have all kinds of denominations on Bermuda and probably have more churches per square mile than anyone. It probably stems from all the immigration we had many years ago. We don't go around preaching religion though. A lot of us keep our faith to ourselves, including me, and there is no religious tension. Any tension is more to do with politics. That's the same in most places, isn't it?

I WAS REALLY CHUFFED WHEN I WAS CHOSEN AS PART OF THE West Ham squad to travel to the USA in May 1969 at the end of the season. This was my very first overseas tour and the North American Soccer League (NASL) was still in its infancy. West Ham were invited, along with Aston Villa, Wolves and two Scottish clubs – Dundee United and Kilmarnock – to play in a close-season tournament.

We started off against Wolves in Baltimore, a game that will stick in the memory, not just because I was playing in the senior team but also because I scored the final West Ham goal in a 3–2 win with four minutes to go. I knew that Ron Greenwood was taking note of my progress but, unfortunately, I took a knock on my ankle against Tottenham Hotspur when I collided with Peter Collins. Tottenham weren't on the tour officially but turned up for a couple of exhibition games. I wish they hadn't. Peter, who was a brute of a centre-half, just came in and cleaned me out. I had to sit out the rest of the tournament and Ron Greenwood allowed me to return to Bermuda – only a ninety-minute flight from where we were.

I remember hobbling off the plane to be met by my parents and telling them that I had to get fit quick – because West Ham and Southampton had agreed to come to Bermuda the following week. It would be the first time that two English First Division sides had played against each other on the island – with a Bermudian playing for one of them.

I was still not 100 per cent fit after the knock I took playing against Spurs but I was desperate to play in front of a home-town crowd. In the end, Southampton were too strong for us. They bossed us around in midfield and soon took the lead, but I managed to equalise twenty minutes later from a cross by John Charles. My ankle was still troubling me though and Trevor Hartley replaced me in the second half.

Trevor Brooking banged one in to put us ahead but Southampton equalised, then grabbed another two just before the end to run out 4–2 winners. Still, I had scored – in fact I was scoring regularly now, virtually every time I played, which augured well for the following season.

After the Southampton game I took the whole West Ham squad, including manager, coaches and directors, to meet my family and friends. My parents put on a reception for about a hundred people at our home in East Shore Road, Somerset. You might have imagined that the guys would have been keen to sample some local culinary delights. Far from it. What they wanted was roast beef and Yorkshire pudding – the very same dish I had grown accustomed to in the UK. I can't remember how my mum felt about that – she probably wanted to make something typically local – but, being the accommodating person she was, and a great cook, she somehow managed to pull it off. The West Ham players loved the house, which was spacious, had four bedrooms, was far bigger than your typical Stepney or Mile End dwelling in those days . . . and was a short walk to the beach.

I made sure all the squad milked what we had to offer: swimming, sunbathing and even some limbo dancing. All these years later, whenever we chat on the phone, Harry Redknapp still raves about that day and he has become a regular visitor to the island in the years since.

It was summer in Bermuda but once again my thoughts were turning towards England and what kind of impact, having turned professional, I could make. I kept myself extremely fit and was determined to break into the West Ham first team. I knew I had the ability.

8

DEBUT AND FIRST GOAL

THE 1969/70 SEASON WAS JUST GETTING UNDER WAY AND ONE morning I went into training, only to be called aside and told to go straight home. What on earth had I done wrong? Had the club changed its mind about me? All kinds of conflicting thoughts went through my mind, but I needn't have worried. Quite the opposite was the case. I was playing that night against Arsenal. We had been beaten 3–1 at home by West Brom just two days earlier and I guess Ron Greenwood, who knew I had been making good progress in the reserves, wanted to freshen things up. To say I had a lump in my throat is an understatement, not least when I saw the team sheet and realised who would be in the starting eleven with me. Bobby was there of course, so was Frank Lampard (whose son would go on to become a Chelsea legend after starting his career at West Ham), Billy Bonds, Martin Peters and Geoff Hurst.

More than 39,000 fans packed into Upton Park, many of them probably bemused – as I'm sure the Arsenal players were too – at the novelty of a black player wearing number 7, although I soon ended up wearing 11. Quite frankly, I didn't give it much thought. When you're young, you think less about that kind of thing. As you get older and more mature, everything comes more into focus. That is probably why I was so shocked as my career progressed to be subjected to so much racial abuse. It's a heavy burden to have to carry. A lot of people just don't understand that. They think you just put on your boots and go out and play. It's more than that.

To be fair, though, I can't recall the Arsenal fans giving me any stick that night. I knew what I was there for and what I had to do. It was the fulfilment of my dreams and, even though I failed to score and we were held 1–1, we hit the woodwork twice and deserved to win. I must have done OK because I found myself playing the next game. 'Clyde Best, the Bermudan making his debut, showed commendable spirit and skill for West Ham,' reported the *Daily Telegraph* the next day. Meanwhile Trevor Smith in the local *Newham Recorder* said it had been his 'biggest fear' that I would get called up following the West Brom defeat. 'Of immense potential, the loose-limbed youngster seemed to me to be far from ready for such a baptism of fire and I had grave misgivings when his name was pencilled in on the team sheet,' he wrote. 'I was wrong.'

One of the tabloid papers concentrated on matters off the field, Desmond Hackett in the *Express* bemoaning the fact that the game was 'marred by petty larceny, fouls and a tiresome procession of thugs being hauled off brawling terraces'. If truth be told, I didn't notice any of it. I was concentrating on the game. How times, thankfully, have changed.

I was – and remain – so grateful to Ron Greenwood for having faith in me. Ron was simply one fantastic human being. He understood the mentality of his players and instilled in us the way he wanted to play. We always remembered what he drilled into us: that when we went on the football field, we had to entertain the crowd. I knew I wanted to play for him from the day I signed for the club. Later I read an article somewhere in which Ron said I was one of the best teenagers he had ever seen in his life. It was a lovely compliment to pay me. Ron was ahead of his time in my opinion, just like Martin Peters. I think he'd have done brilliantly if he'd managed on the continent because he wanted his teams to play with control and technique. He always said, 'Think of the fans, they're the ones who pay your wages.'

After I played against Arsenal my confidence started to grow even more, so much so that a couple of weeks later, on 3 September, I scored my first West Ham goal in a 4–2 League Cup second-round win against Halifax Town. Obviously it felt great, but it was the league I wanted to conquer and I already had my eyes set on a trip to Old Trafford at the end of September. Manchester United had recently won the European Cup and I listened breathlessly as Ron Greenwood read out the names of those who would travel north. When mine was read out, I had to pinch myself at the thought of coming up against the likes of George Best and Bobby Charlton.

In those days, unlike the luxury travel of today, players often made their own way to the station (maybe Euston or King's Cross) to catch the train for matches against northern teams like United, Liverpool or Everton. Normally, there would be one or two carriages reserved for us in first class. Supporters often travelled on the same train as the players, with a day return costing around £4. But some things haven't changed and many fans followed us on supporter coaches with different departure points in the East End of London – e.g. Gillett Avenue in East Ham, Broadway in Barking, the Grasshopper Coach Station in Mayville Road, Ilford, and from the Merry Fiddler in Dagenham.

It was the first time I had ever been to Old Trafford and it brought me out in goose bumps. The stadium was filled to capacity with an official attendance of 58,579. I remember, as I looked round the stadium, thinking that was the equivalent of the entire population of Bermuda. The game didn't exactly pan out as I'd hoped and United ran out 5–2 winners. They were in front after only five minutes when Francis Burns headed in a John Aston corner. Five minutes later, Georgie Best – who else? – slammed in a Willie Morgan cross and we were two down with still another eighty minutes left to play.

In the 25th minute, I helped reduce the deficit as I swung in a corner which Geoff Hurst nodded home for 2–1. It was quite unusual for big centre-forwards to take corners but whenever I played on the right, rather than down the middle, I often took them. You have to remember that for much of that period, Hurst was the number 9. Soon after Geoff's goal I so nearly scored an equaliser when I blasted in a shot that Alex Stepney somehow managed to claw away. After the interval Bobby Charlton made it 3–1, but we were by no means out of it. Just like against Arsenal, the United players and fans saw this little-known black player from a far-off land get his head down and prove he could play on any stage. Receiving the ball on the right, I strode past United left-back John Fitzpatrick, glanced up, saw Geoff Hurst running towards goal, and crossed for Geoff to get that famous head on the ball and halve the deficit once more.

Any hopes of nicking a point were wiped out by the more illustrious Best as George finished off an in-swinger, then Brian Kidd killed us off as he slid home a John Aston cross.

It was the first time I had played against Georgie and how quickly I understood why he had gained such an incredible reputation. George and I went on to share a healthy respect for one another. He was an awesome player, probably in the top three in the world at the time along with Pelé and Johan Cruyff. I always used to tell George that when I went to Old Trafford it was his stage but whenever he came to Upton Park it was mine. I'll never forget one game in particular, during the 1971/72 season, when United murdered us and George scored a hat-trick. He himself said later that his second goal that day was one of his best ever, cutting in and beating several players, even though he was off-balance, and hitting it with his weaker foot. He was irresistible and I felt sorry for both our full-backs. On his day he could do that to anyone.

People say a lot of things about how George conducted himself off the pitch. I know that he was one for the ladies and had somewhat of a bad-boy reputation, not least when it came to partying. But to me, he was a fantastic character. Like me, George came over to England at a young age without his family. Plus, we had the same surname. That's where the similarity ended because I didn't have his looks, let alone his mesmerising feet. And of course I was a different colour. A lot of people in my opinion tried to lead George astray. Perhaps he was too impressionable but he had a wonderfully soft side that maybe made him do things he shouldn't have. What I mean by that is if you are not a really tough individual you can get caught up in that kind of stuff. The fact is George was a diamond. He once came to Bermuda with Manchester United and, although he was obviously recognised, he wasn't mobbed in the same way he often was in England. That's the way Bermudians are.

Even though we lost 5–2 on that September day, I was pleased with my performance, all the more so when the *Daily Express* headlined their match report: 'Best Boys Share Glory'. Another newspaper reported that I had given United centre-half Ian Ure 'a most uncomfortable afternoon' and 'with a rare mixture of strength and subtlety looked as though with a little more experience he could provide Hurst with some much-needed support'.

Bobby Moore echoed these sentiments. Bobby used to write a weekly column in one of the London newspapers and after the Manchester United game, he wrote:

THE ACID TEST

If George Best was at his most brilliant we could derive tremendous encouragement from the performance of our own Best, Clyde. It was difficult at times to remember that Clyde, for all his size and power, is still only a teenager and virtually as yet a novice in the professional game.

They were lovely words from a lovely man, but I was still awaiting my first league goal. As a striker you know that if you are playing well the goals will come, so it didn't really bother me. I didn't have to wait much longer. Saturday, 4 October 1969, will always linger long in the memory. In my sixth game for the Hammers, I scored twice that day, the first from a cross by Trevor Brooking after selling a gorgeous dummy, the second from a Geoff Hurst pass, both in the first fifteen minutes. Trevor nicked a third goal near the end, with Steve Kindon grabbing a consolation for visitors Burnley.

You could say that's when my career really took off. My name was all over the following Monday morning sports sections of the national newspapers. The story was as much about how someone my size had so much speed as about my goals. 'Boy Best Bags Two', trumpeted one headline. 'Best helps them forget Peters', read another. 'Secret weapon Best baffles Burnley plan', said the local *Newham Recorder*, whose reporter Trevor Smith summed up my performance thus: 'His verve and subtle touches continually belied the unbelievably brief professional experience behind him. Barely a year's professional experience of English pro football . . . and he is taking on defences with the panache of the other Best.' Praise indeed! As it happens, I had been wearing Martin Peters' number 11 shirt. In those days, shirts were 1 to 11, not like today when anything goes and you sometimes can't even identify the player by the number he's wearing. Martin had been dropped by Ron Greenwood and had applied for a transfer. It was a massive story at the time. After all, this was the player who could pass with either foot, was good in the air and difficult to mark because of his movement. And this was the player, remember, described by Alf Ramsey as being ten years ahead of his time.

I couldn't allow all this to distract me from the task in hand and was delighted to read one report which described me as 'the tall, dazzling, 18-year-old Best!' I phoned my dad in Bermuda and told him about the headline. I also reported that the *London Evening Standard* had nominated me as Man of the Match.

*

JUST AFTER THE SEASON STARTED I MOVED FOR GOOD TO THE Charles' – Jessie and her two West Ham-playing sons, John and Clive. There were originally nine children in the Charles family but most had grown up and left home by the time I moved in. John, whose father was a merchant seaman from Grenada – and Jessie's third husband – was the first black footballer (half-black to be precise) to play for West Ham in 1963, while Clive, the youngest of the nine, was about seven months younger than me and had been training with the club from the age of twelve. John admitted to being part of a strong drinking culture that existed at West Ham in the 1960s, but I won't have a word said against him. They were all Hammers through and through and, like thousands of East Enders, lived in a terraced house in a working-class neighbourhood, with a living room and kitchen downstairs, bedrooms and bathroom upstairs, and a small garden outside. There was a lovely, caring atmosphere in the Charles household. If Jessie was like a second mother to me, Clive was almost like a brother.

I paid Mrs Charles five pounds a week for my lodgings, an eighth of what I was earning. By the time my income tax came off, plus National Insurance etc., I was left with only half that amount. The United Kingdom is a heavily taxed country, but the National Health Service means that health care is available to every citizen. The system is the envy of many and while there has always been controversy about whether the NHS is efficient enough, it is far preferable than having to pay private health insurance. But it has to be paid for through taxes – and single working people are hit hardest because they have fewer 'deductibles' than those with families.

I've said before that I was more than happy with £40 a week but that's a far cry from what players earn today and the transfer fees involved. It's all become crazy. The most that I ever earned at West Ham was about £180 a week. I'm not complaining – it was far more than the average worker managed. And with the pound worth about $2.50 back then, it would have gone a long way in Bermuda. Naturally, I felt I was living somewhat of a privileged life. Hardly a day went by when I didn't remind myself of that. I knew how fortunate I was, though I have to say wages have always been pretty good in Bermuda as long as I can remember. There were probably some people earning more than me at the high end, those who worked, for instance, in international business. But nobody flaunts their wealth. We've always been low key in that respect. We don't indulge in who makes how much. I have no idea, for instance, how much my dad earned in the prison service, but it must have been a fair whack to look after all of us!

Having said all that, today the wages some players earn has gone mad. Footballers are like movie stars. They earn more in six weeks than most mortals do in a lifetime. Compared to this day and age, what I was paid at West Ham was peanuts. When you see a young man like Raheem Sterling being sold for almost £50 million, it's mind-boggling. Sterling had only been at Liverpool for a couple of seasons, and going for that amount of money to Manchester City seemed really strange to me. He more or less turned his back on Liverpool. They are a huge club in world football, but really I guess that's the nature of the beast right now. If there are good young English players, the price goes up. Sterling is probably in the top ten, and City had the money. He can certainly play and has been touted as one of the best young players in Europe. That's quite a mantle to assume. What if his form starts deteriorating? Does he then become a flop?

As for the money, I don't know how much the boy takes home, but in my day I couldn't even dream about what some of these kids earn. In my opinion, some of the money now in the game should be passed up the generations. That might sound odd, but I tell people all the time that when you look at football today and the money in it, and then you consider the hundreds of past players who never really got much at all, you'd think there might be a scheme whereby some of it goes into a fund to help them. That's what they do in the NFL in the United States. It's a much fairer system than we have in England. I'm not saying this because of my own situation. I'm as comfortable as I want to be in retirement, thank you very much. I neither have too much nor too little. But there are loads of ex-players who deserve to be financially recognised when they have hung up their boots. You may ask why? The answer is simple: without the older players, there'd be no new players. It's a source of disappointment to me that there is no mechanism for funds to filter through to the older generation. Look at people like Stanley Matthews, Tom Finney and what they've done for football.

When you see what they and their families got from the game compared to the kids today, it's disproportionate. Some of these kids are still barely on the fringes of the first team and making thirty grand a week. The older guys never made that in a lifetime. It would be nice if the powers that be could devise some kind of method to reward some of the older players or, if they are no longer with us, to look after their families. Take Jimmy Greaves, who not so long ago had a massive stroke. These guys need to be looked after. With the huge television money now flowing through the game, there's more than enough there for everybody.

I WAS SETTLING IN WELL, THOUGH STILL COMING TO TERMS with the sheer size of London. Thank goodness for the Charles and the Dexter families. I considered them my lucky charms. Without them to keep my feet on the ground, Lord knows how I'd have ended up. Perhaps as one of those panel-beaters. To be all that way from home and be so well looked after, it's a testament to both families. I still miss Jessie so much. She wouldn't have a bad word said about me and vice versa.

What no one could acclimatise me to was the miserable weather, which seemed to go on for weeks on end. I remember seeing my first snowfall and not being able to work it out. It was when we were at Portman Road getting ready to play Ipswich. I stood and watched these small white flakes falling gently all around me and I was fascinated by them. The rest of the team stood and watched me watching the snow. They could hardly stand up they were laughing so much.

Christmas was rapidly approaching but I had no time for homesickness. I was holding on to my first-team place at West Ham and we had games all over the festive season, a very English custom that took a while for me to get used to; foreign players, even today, find it really hard to deal with – or some of them do. Understandably they don't get it that while much of Europe shuts down over Christmas and New Year, in England and Scotland the crowds are bigger than ever.

People have been talking for years about a winter break in terms of improving the fortunes of the national team, but is it not the case that the number of foreign players also has an effect? I feel quite strongly about this. You could argue I'm being hypocritical because I was one of the trailblazers, but you can't have players coming into the country all the time and displacing those who are already there. That's not right. Eventually it's bound to affect your national team. Look at England's over the past 25 years. When were they last a really formidable force? Maybe not since Euro 96. Why? Simply because English kids don't get a chance to play for top clubs on a regular basis.

I know it's unrealistic in these days of freedom of movement in Europe, but I would still favour quotas: a set number of foreign players on the field at any one time. When I played at Feyenoord towards the end of my career, you were only allowed three. Indeed, that was the case in many European leagues until the 1990s. If we want the English national team to be successful we must reintroduce quotas. The game is the best teacher. At some clubs there are ten foreigners in the first team – that's just ludicrous. I'm all in favour of foreign players getting an opportunity, but it's all about balance. I'm really impressed by what clubs like Tottenham are trying to do now. Players like Harry Kane, Dele Alli and Eric Dier are keeping foreigners out of the side.

MRS CHARLES HAD HER CHRISTMAS TREE UP IN THE LIVING ROOM and Christmas cards strung along the top of the fireplace. In Bermuda we decorate inside and outside our houses over the Christmas season. Lights, lights and more lights. We string multicoloured lights all over the trees and bushes in our gardens as well as all round the eaves of the houses. We line the paths to our houses with lights: we also wrap lights round our cedars and palmetto palm trees so that our homes and gardens look really festive.

I was not the only Bermudian who would be spending Christmas away from home. My brother Carlton was studying and working in London. It was a great comfort to me to have him close by. I was in touch with many Bermudians working or studying in UK at that time, including Sinclair White, Freddy Wade, Michael Scott, Larry Scott, Eddie Robinson, Dennis Hart, Suzie Darrell, Morris Francis and Chick Simons. Let me take you through them. Sinclair I befriended at high school. He joined the police force in Bermuda after his career. Freddy came to England to study law but his true calling was politics and he went on to become leader of our Progressive Labour Party (PLP). Michael and Larry were also studying law and came from the same neighbourhood as me. Eddie was into cooking big-time and ended up working as a prison officer back home, where he used his culinary skills to good effect. Dennis was big on motor mechanics, Suzie was in the medical field and Chick was into telecommunications – just like my brother. They lived in West Norwood. If only I could remember what Morris was in England for. I think he was studying in England. Sorry, Morris! Sometimes when we got together, we'd eat traditional Bermuda food like rice and peas, but our cuisine is actually not much different to that in England – lots of steak, chicken and fish.

Of course, there was no Internet in those days, so no email or online newspapers. Although I talked to my dad regularly by phone it was nice to hear Bermudian accents in the depths of an English winter. Others I saw regularly were Fred and Charlotte Ming – Fred was in the culinary trade and Charlotte was a schoolteacher – Herman Basden (who came to England to study transportation), Adrienne Tucker, Cheryl Smith, Ellie Wainwright, Lynn Bulford, Jackie Talbot, Lydia Perinchief, Pam Brangman, Marlette Butterfield, Althea Minors, Bradford Trott and Francis Jeffries. I know this may once again just sound like a long list of unknown people, but they weren't unknown to me. You have to understand how good it was to get together with them all at one time or another. It was like a home from home, a comfort zone in a way. I often got homesick on a Sunday when there wasn't much to do. It was quite tough and these people helped pull me through many, many a time. I remember Adrienne Tucker well because my sister married her brother. Like many of the others in the list above, Adrienne was studying nursing. With Bermuda being a British colony, we studied the English curriculum so it made sense for a lot of people to go to university in the UK. These days a lot of Bermudians go to the USA and Canada, but back then most went to England. University was pretty accessible, but you had to get the school grades first. It was never going to be for me, though. I chose football instead.

Sometimes we used to meet at the Tam O'Shanter Steakhouse in Leicester Square for an evening out – or in the Black Lion pub or Baker's Arms closer to 'home' in the East End. I will always remember and appreciate their support. I used to get asked for tickets all the time and was willing to oblige. It was good to have people of my own nationality cheering me on, however I played.

*

IN LATE MAY 1970, ONCE THE 1969/70 SEASON WAS OVER, MAN-chester United flew to my country to play exhibition games against a Bermuda Select XI. I was given special permission by West Ham to be a guest player for Bermuda and thousands of fans flocked into our National Stadium.

It would be the first time in almost two years that Randy Horton and I had played in the same team together. We were renewing the striking partnership that had caused panic in opposing defences back in the late 60s, albeit at domestic level.

What a fright we gave United as we threw caution to the wind – only to fall behind after eighteen minutes when Tony Fitzpatrick got on the end of a cross. He was the provider fifteen minutes later when Willie Morgan slipped the ball past our goalie.

A quarter of an hour after the interval, Randy thundered home a scorcher and Gary Darrell started to find Randy and myself with some neat through-balls. One of his passes reached Randy, who quickly moved the ball to George Brangman. George's volley gave the United keeper no chance.

United's Fitzpatrick stretched their lead once more, however, with a shot that went through a flurry of legs. The Bermuda crowd was loving this end-to-end action and United sealed their win with a fine dipping shot our keeper could do little about. Still, our heads were held high and United's manager Wilf McGuinness, as well as the Bermuda national coach at the time, Bernd Fischer, congratulated us on an inspired performance. McGuinness also commented on how good the playing surface was, even though this was hardly Old Trafford.

Our confidence was high and we were determined to do just as well against our next visitors, Celtic, the first team in the UK to have won the European Cup in 1967. It was another 'Bermudaful' summer's evening in front of another packed house at the National Stadium.

In Celtic's line-up was Lou Macari. Because we had done so well against United, all of us putting ourselves in the shop window, we thought we stood a good chance of causing an upset. After all, Celtic had travelled to Bermuda without established stars such as Jimmy Johnstone, Tommy Gemmell, Bertie Auld and Steve Chalmers.

Instead, they tore us apart.

We were down 4–0 at half-time, Vic Davidson scoring three. Willie Wallace notched a couple after the interval – one a penalty – before Bobby Lennox rattled in their final goal. Randy Horton, who came on at half-time, pulled one back near the end, but in truth we were overwhelmed by a Celtic side that exposed our frailties and played an all-out attacking game with five forwards – sometimes it seemed to be more.

We could not find an answer to the lightning speed with which their midfielders suddenly became part of a five-pronged attack. Nevertheless, it was a wonderful experience for us and we enjoyed the whole occasion.

Celtic had brought several youth players to give them some exposure. One of them caught my eye with his reading of the game, his excellent passing and overall football sense. He would go on to be a prolific striker for Celtic and then Liverpool before becoming the Liverpool manager. You guessed it. The youngster's name was Kenny Dalglish.

A FEW MONTHS LATER, JUST AFTER THE BEGINNING OF THE 1970/71 season, West Ham were invited to play in an exhibition match in the United States against Santos of Brazil, a flying visit between a home game against Newcastle and an away match at Huddersfield. The Americans made a big deal of it. In one of our match programmes, Clive Toye, then the administration director of the United States Soccer League, was quoted: 'We want to show off the best there is. Santos and West Ham are renowned for the calibre of their football. This match would fill any stadium either side of the Atlantic. West Ham against Santos – Pelé against Moore – is a game they will flock to see. I can think of no better ambassadors for football than Santos and West Ham.'

Quite a billing to live up to. We left on a Sunday, played the game on the following Wednesday and were back by the Saturday. The fixture, in front of 22,000, took place at Randall's Island stadium in New York. Everyone wanted to be a part of it given the name of the Santos skipper, the most famous footballer on the planet. Like millions of others, I had seen Pelé on television yet now I was to be given the opportunity of physically lining up against him.

We winged our way to New York, leaving behind a typical late September day in London – rain and cloud. When we got off the plane at JFK the temperature was 80°F – with humidity to match. We felt as if we were in a steam bath. In the event, a packed stadium turned up to see the great man open the scoring in the nineteenth minute when midfielder Lima slipped a through-ball into him and he made no mistake with a thunderbolt our defence could do nothing about.

Anything Pelé could do, another black striker – though a far less skilful and prestigious one – could do too. Fighting back, we levelled ten minutes later courtesy of yours truly. I had the ball at my feet about thirty yards out, looked up, saw a tiny opening between a ruck of Santos defenders – and battered it. The goalie saw it too late and dived unsuccessfully to his right. The crowd were loving it.

Pelé, being Pelé, manufactured another wonder goal but we were not over-awed by the South Americans. Once again, I matched him goal for goal. This time I collected a ball out on the right, strode into the box and let fly. We were on level terms again and that's how the game stood at half-time.

In the second half Santos threw everything at us and we had to defend desperately, but we hung on for a draw on a burning New York evening that sapped our strength. I was bursting with pride at the end. I was only nineteen years old yet had scored a brace against a team that contained the world's greatest talent and a whole lot of other awesome names, such as Carlos Alberto. You can't get much better than that. I was even more delighted when Pelé autographed a picture of himself for me. I still have that picture all these years later at home in Bermuda. I'll never part with it.

Several years later, I was to play in the same team as Pelé when I was invited to go on a tour of Japan and Europe as a guest with Cosmos while I was with Tampa Bay. How many players have lining up alongside Pelé on their CV? We first played Paris Saint-Germain and the Belgian side Antwerp and ended up losing 3–1 to them both. We then moved on to Japan, where we played a score-less draw in Kobe against West Japan All-Stars and then drew 2–2 in Tokyo against East Japan All-Stars. Pelé and I may have had different mother tongues but I can honestly say he never once pulled rank, he never once came across as superior. What is it about some of these superstars that keeps them humble and down to earth? Bobby Moore was the same.

Roughly six months before the Santos game, and arguably the biggest story of 1970 as far as West Ham were concerned, Martin Peters left the club after being controversially exchanged for Jimmy Greaves. The deal was done on transfer deadline day, the forms rushed to the relevant authorities by Ron Greenwood, who drove 240 miles to deliver the papers in person, shortly before midnight. Jimmy was a brilliant goal scorer but he was thirty, whereas Martin was four years younger and certain to be chosen for the upcoming World Cup squad in Mexico. The fact is Martin had suffered a loss of form while Jimmy already had 57 caps for England, scoring 41 goals in the process, a total exceeded at the time only by Bobby Charlton.

By the time Jimmy was 21 he had scored 100 goals in English top-flight football. The problem was that he was no longer 21. When he arrived at West Ham he was past his peak and, although he scored twice on his debut for us in a 5-1 win over Manchester City, many supporters felt that we were getting the 'thin end of the wedge', so to speak, and made it clear how they felt. So did the local newspapers. I felt differently. Everyone knew Jimmy had a chronic drink problem but I never once questioned him about it. I was always very attentive in his company in terms of learning off him, and felt the other side of his life was none of my business.

You may have thought that, being a fellow striker, I would not be too happy about a legend like Jimmy coming to the club, but I took the view that the more competition for striking places, the better. I just wanted to learn, to improve, to enhance my skills – and who better to learn from than one of England's most famous forwards?

At the beginning of that 1970/71 season, therefore, I felt great. I enjoyed the training, I got on well with everyone at the club, I had marvellous digs with the Charles family and I felt really positive about the coming campaign. Perhaps it was just as well that my teenage brain could not imagine some of the problems looming on the horizon.

9

THE BLACKPOOL FIASCO

FOOTBALL IS INDEED 'A FUNNY OLD GAME', AS THE OLD CLICHÉ goes. There I was, a teenager playing for West Ham one week against the famous Pelé in New York City – then winging my way back across the Atlantic and lining up for a Tuesday night South East Counties League game against Watford at our training ground.

It was Ron Greenwood's way of making sure I did not let things go to my head, that I kept my feet on the ground. I was still ten years younger than some of the first-team players at West Ham so I would be included in the first team one week, and the Football Combination the next. Everyone likes to play all the time but it was invaluable experience for me.

Around Christmas 1970 we were hovering around the relegation zone having not won a home game since October. Yet despite being in and out of the team I was still banging in the goals and it seemed only a matter of time before I became a regular, never again having to worry about playing in the reserves in front of the proverbial two men and a dog.

Then came 'that' day in Blackpool. The date sticks in my mind like a leaden weight I can't shake off: 2 January 1971. Blackpool is located in the northwest corner of England, facing the Irish Sea. I have to admit that I was never sure exactly where some of these towns actually were. It is even further north than Liverpool and Manchester and is what the English like to call a holiday resort city, where families go in the summer to visit the Pleasure Beach and famous tower and pier.

But there was nothing pleasurable about it for me. I'd say it was one of my darkest periods. Ron Greenwood was always a man of principle and expected his players to behave the same way – on and off the pitch. He was adamant that no stain would be left on the club during his tenure.

West Ham had been drawn away to the Seasiders in the third round of the FA Cup. Despite being only two places below us in the league, they were considered very much the underdogs and it would have caused a mighty shock if they could tumble the Hammers. We had travelled up from Euston station on the Friday, a train journey of about five hours. We arrived late afternoon, it was snowing and the first news we got was that the game might have to be postponed because the pitch was iced up and the weather was awful. There isn't much to do in Blackpool in the middle of winter so after dinner in the hotel we sat chatting in the lounge, intending to have an early night. But then, we reasoned, if the game was going to be off, what harm was there in whipping out for a couple of hours?

Myself, Jimmy Greaves, Bobby Moore and Brian Dear got talking to some members of a television crew. They told us they were going to visit a nightclub run by Brian London, the former British heavyweight boxing champion. Bobby knew Brian so we all decided to go along. It was only to be a short visit to say hello. I remember having a couple of ginger beers and lime and catching a taxi back to the hotel, arriving after midnight. It didn't seem that big a deal. But a few hours later, the proverbial shit, if you'll excuse my use of language, hit the fan. Next morning, instead of getting on the train back to London, we were informed that the game was on. We could hardly believe it. When we got to the stadium at Bloomfield Road, the pitch was rock hard but had been declared playable.

To this day, I tell everyone about Tony Green's performance for Blackpool whenever the subject is raised. The surface was at times like ice but he reminded me of a ballerina. The Seasiders launched themselves at us from the first whistle. A typical northern mist hovered over the bone-hard pitch and the home fans rubbed their hands in anticipation of us being a soft touch. Blackpool had a new and enthusiastic coach, Bob Stokoe. If his name sounds familiar, he was the Sunderland manager who, a couple of years later, famously ran across the Wembley pitch to applaud his heroic players after their 1973 FA Cup final upset victory over Leeds United.

Geoff Hurst had been ruled out of the game and I took his place, although it's fair to say I didn't have one of my better games. I remember Green taking control of midfield from the start, then opening the scoring and adding a second before half-time. He mastered the elements better than anyone. We just couldn't get near him. By the end Blackpool had added a healthy dose of salt to our wounds to complete a 4–0 rout. Our failure was magnified by the fact that it was recorded by the *Match of the Day* cameras.

Blackpool's assistant manager Jimmy Meadows was quoted afterwards as saying Bobby Moore was 'highly over-rated' and the 'worst defender in the world'. It was nonsense, of course, and Blackpool apologised for the comment, but it was a measure of the euphoria surrounding the Seasiders' famous win. And there was worse to come.

If it had been a long train journey north on the Friday, the Saturday night return journey seemed to go on for an eternity. There wasn't much conversation from anyone. We got back to Euston very late, retrieved our cars from the parking lot and went home. We had been soundly beaten by a team languishing at the foot of the First Division, a team that would go on to be relegated at the end of that season. As we drove through the darkened London streets, past Poplar and Whitechapel, we tried to put it out of our minds and concentrate on the next game coming up in the league.

Little did we know that our troubles were only just beginning.

Someone had leaked the story to the press that we were all sitting in a nightclub in Blackpool till the wee hours before a critical cup tie. The tabloids went wild with the story. Ron went bonkers and reportedly wanted to sack us, only to be dissuaded from doing so by the West Ham board. Our chairman Reg Pratt questioned us then fined us all two weeks' wages, the maximum allowed under FA rules. For me this meant a total of about £150, a lot of money back then.

Greaves, Moore and I were all dropped from the first team, but I can promise you all these years later that I never got up to anything. I just went along for the company. It was common knowledge that drinking was not my thing. It still isn't today. I only had soft drinks, but it was yet another mistake I had to learn from as an impressionable teenager. In fairness, all the senior guys spoke up for me and told Ron Greenwood that I hadn't been drinking. Sadly, Jimmy and Brian would soon be on their way out, but Ron Greenwood didn't hold the incident against me.

Brian Dear fared particularly badly and was soon named as a *reserve* for the subsequent reserve game against Bristol Rovers. He left the club within weeks of the incident, while Jimmy Greaves retired a few months later. I suppose I got off relatively unscathed compared to the others. I heard later that Ron Greenwood's relationship with Bobby Moore was never the same again. Bobby, as you know, was sold to Fulham in 1974.

On top of that, we were not that far above Blackpool in the league – we finished third from bottom that season – and some West Ham fans were still fiercely critical of the deal which had seen Martin Peters leave for Spurs.

Remember, too, that worldwide communications were not what they are in the 21st century. In Bermuda, weekend papers from England were only delivered on the flight the following Tuesday. What if my parents found out about the incident before I had a chance to tell them myself? I had to call. Luckily I was able to reassure them that my role in the incident had been blown out of all proportion by the tabloid press. In addition Mrs Charles, bless her, personally wrote to my mother to let her know I was innocent. Having said all that, even today I still feel the guys didn't do anything that bad. The thing is, when you are a professional footballer and get caught for breaking rules, you invariably get punished.

Things were not going too well on the field, either. Some of the banners on the terracing read: 'Greenwood Must Go' and 'We Have Had Enough'. Indeed, four weeks after the Blackpool fiasco, Derby County came to Upton Park and 'hammered' us 4–1. We were deep in the relegation zone by this time and neither Jimmy Greaves nor I could get a regular game, with

preferred up front.

Right at the end of February, minus Jimmy Greaves, Brian Dear and myself, the first team again assembled at Euston station to catch the morning train to Blackpool, this time on league business. There would be no repeat of the January mauling and no repeat of the nightclub escapades, although Bobby Moore was relegated to the substitutes' bench. We managed a 1–1 draw to partially ease our relegation worries, Geoff Hurst netting a spot kick. A few weeks later, Blackpool finished 22nd and bottom of the table while we ended up 20th, narrowly avoiding the drop in the days of two up, two down. In a way, I was glad I didn't have to make another long trip north. I was growing tired of those train journeys.

10

TOUGHEST GAME OF MY LIFE

AT THE END OF THE SEASON, IN MAY 1971, I JETTED HOME TO Bermuda – but there was little thought of relaxation on my mind. Once again I was determined not to slack off or put on any weight during the close season. Every Monday morning in Bermuda, cruise ships from New York and Florida disgorge thousands of passengers in Hamilton and St George's. Our beaches are crowded with locals and tourists alike, soaking up the sun and swimming in our crystal-clear blue waters.

I hardly noticed them as I put myself through a rigorous training schedule each day, determined to stay in peak condition. I felt that I had not been at my best during the previous season – perhaps it was lack of confidence at being thrown into the cauldron of English top-flight football at too early an age. There is little time to dwell on the ball in England. Defenders often play man-to-man marking, sticking like glue to the strikers; it means that as a forward you have only than a split second to get away. This may sound true of anywhere in the world, but it isn't. In England it's a different kettle of fish entirely from elsewhere. The game is faster. That's why some of the foreign players who come over to England find it difficult to stay consistent: because of the pace of the game. Look at Leicester City's amazing 2015/16 season. I heard many pundits talk about a new way of playing. It made me laugh because what Leicester were doing was playing the old-fashioned British way – and doing it better than anyone else. Running their socks off and squeezing the opposition.

We were set for a tour of the USA in June and I knew that Ron Greenwood would be watching everyone closely to find his best team for the following season. I certainly didn't do my chances any harm as I scored thirteen times against teams like Necaxa of Mexico and Rot-Weiss, a West German side, as we travelled between Los Angeles and Seattle. I scored with both feet, with my head – in fact every time I had a shot it seemed to end up in the back of the net. I was playing alongside Geoff Hurst in many of the games; we were reading each other well and it gave my confidence a much-needed boost.

On the way back to the UK we stopped off in Bermuda to play a friendly against PHC, the triple crown champions that year. The lads were firmly focused on providing entertainment and we romped to a 7–0 win. I can honestly say that PHC never stopped trying for the entire game. Guys like Jimmy Parsons, Dale Russell and Ellie Wilson gave everything they had and were unlucky with several of their shots. But they were up against a well-oiled West Ham machine that night. Two of our youngsters really stood out. The first was a talented young winger called John Ayris, who ran the PHC defence ragged. The other was a young Nigerian who had played with me in the reserves. His control and movement on and off the ball were a joy to behold. His name was Ade Coker.

That summer went by in a flash and suddenly it was time for my parents to drive me once again to the airport to catch yet another flight back to England. All the players were fighting fit, we had a very successful American tour under our belt, and mid-August could not come quickly enough. Or so we thought.

We lost our first two home games of the 1971/72 season as West Bromwich Albion beat us 1–0 and Derby County put two past us without reply four days later. We were still in the third week of August when we travelled to play Nottingham Forest and lost again. Then Ipswich Town visited the Boleyn Ground and we eked out a dull 0–0 draw.

It wasn't supposed to have started like that and we were all in a state of shock. I imagine Ron Greenwood felt under some pressure but if that's true he never showed it. He was a cool, calm character and knew his own ability.

Our first break came when Everton visited. Bobby Moore took a free kick and I outjumped the opposition defence to nod home. It was our first goal of the season and to say that we were relieved is a massive understatement. The win gave us a massive boost, so much so that when Coventry came calling we hammered them 4–0 with yours truly bagging two and Geoff and Pop Robson grabbing one apiece. John Ayris had a marvellous game that afternoon, turning the Coventry defence inside out and setting up two of the goals.

September became a good month for me. I scored seven goals in eight games, including two crackers – one with the head against Chelsea when they visited us. We were not so lucky when we played Manchester United at Old Trafford the following week. The largest crowd of the day in England – 53,000 – saw the 'other Best' outshine me with a sublime hat-trick as we went down 4–2, with Bobby Charlton grabbing the other one. Still, we played our part in a fast-moving, entertaining game and I'm pleased to say that the 'Bermuda "Bye" Best' scored.

The *Evening Standard* is the most widely read newspaper in London and at the end of September I received a phone call from one of their editors naming me as the *Evening Standard* Footballer of the Month. I was thrilled, especially considering that I was still only twenty. The *Standard* reporters asked Ron Greenwood about me and he said that I had become 'a bit more aggressive' compared to the previous season. Perhaps I had, but I had never consciously thought about it.

What I do know is that I had formed a very effective striking partnership with Geoff Hurst. 'Clyde has taken a lot of the weight off me. He gets on with it. He likes to run and take defenders on,' Geoff said at the time. 'He holds people off as well and his biggest assets are his speed, shooting and heading.' Geoff finished his remarks with: 'It's nearer the truth to say he has had an influence on the team as a whole.'

Quite a compliment from someone who scored the winning goal in a World Cup final. For me, Geoff was one of, if not the best, centre-forwards in the world in that era. He taught me a lot about playing as the target man, playing with my back to goal.

As well as receiving a beautifully engraved silver plate I was presented with two huge magnums of Lanson Black Label champagne. I still have that plate at home along with my other trophies. The champagne I shared with the rest of the lads.

*

ALL OF THE GAMES WERE HARD AND FAST– EVERY SINGLE ONE. It was the same then as it is today. The English First Division, like its successor the Premier League that was founded in 1992, had no 'pushover' teams. Each provincial club offered a stern challenge and this was an era in which both Derby and Nottingham Forest won league titles. But some games left you totally wrecked.

Looking back over my career, there is one game that stands out as the most exhausting 90 minutes – or 120 minutes as it eventually turned out – of my footballing life. It was against Leeds United at Elland Road in the League Cup. At the beginning of October we had battled to a bruising 0–0 draw at Upton Park. It was a fast, pulsating game in which neither side was able to deliver a knockout punch.

Leeds were one of the most successful teams in Europe at the time. They were always in the top three or four in the league and had just won the Inter-Cities Fairs Cup. The team was packed with international players. Who that saw it can ever forget watching their titanic battle against Glasgow Celtic in the semi-final of the European Cup in April 1970? More than 100,000 spectators had packed into Hampden Park in Glasgow to watch Celtic narrowly edge home 2–1 to proceed to the final. Leeds also had a reputation for being hard as nails, but that never bothered me. And it actually didn't bother that many of my peers as far as I can remember. You see, training was different back then, lots of hard running. These days players seem to drop like flies in terms of getting injured. I believe it has a lot to do with training techniques and physical fitness. All this small-sided stuff, running from cone to cone, does not build your stamina up.

Once again, the West Ham players assembled at Euston station to make the journey north for the League Cup replay, knowing it would be another hard-fought game. Understatement of the year. They came at us like an express train right from the kick-off, moving the ball quickly, probing, trying to get it to Allan 'Sniffer' Clarke. We weren't exactly sitting back either, and tested their defence whenever we could, a defence comprising Terry Cooper, Jackie Charlton, Norman 'Bites Yer Legs' Hunter and Paul Reaney, all of them seasoned internationals.

The first half was played at whirlwind speed on a pitch that became more cut up and muddy as the game progressed. These were the kind of pitches that characterised the era but it didn't bother me simply because, even in that state, they were better than some of the pitches I had been used to playing on at home. Can you imagine how many tricks players of my generation, having coped with those kinds of conditions, would have been able to perform on some of today's smooth surfaces? What would George Best, Bobby Moore and Geoff Hurst have been able to do if they played now? They'd be doubly as devastating as they were.

Anyway, there was no letting up in the second half. If anything the tempo increased. I could feel every muscle in my legs and thighs begin to burn. After ninety minutes it was still all-square and we had to play an extra fifteen minutes each way.

I looked round at the rest of the lads as Ron Greenwood came onto the pitch to organise us for extra time. They all looked as exhausted as me. I just wanted to get extra time started before every muscle in my body seized up.

The tempo slowed but Leeds were still coming forward like a battering ram, thwarted by Bobby Moore, who was having a terrific match. Bobby was all over the place, not just orchestrating things at the back but trying to set up chances for me and Geoff. The game seesawed from one end to the other, neither side willing to give an inch. I could see the exhaustion on everyone's faces. We were all utterly knackered.

Then, suddenly, the breakthrough happened. Roughly ten minutes into the first period of extra time, Harry Redknapp played a ball into the Leeds box from the right side. I outjumped Jack Charlton and Norman Hunter and scored with a glancing header.

How we hung on for the next twenty minutes or so I do not know and never will. The goal gave us new momentum, however, and Bryan Robson hit the post with a few minutes left on the clock. Boy, did we all enjoy our bath after the game! I could feel every muscle in my body, from my toes to my forehead, screaming and protesting – but we had done it. We had beaten one of Europe's best teams on their own patch.

I was especially pleased for our travelling fans who had made that long train journey north to support us. They now had to trek back home and would not arrive in London until the small hours. At least the players had a more civilised plan, a hotel having been booked for us before returning next morning.

Geoff and I were now a solid partnership but it had taken a lot of toil to get to this point. The good thing about going to England when I did is that I had started off in the youth team. I was no big star, I was a teenager living in the East End of London and that's the way people treated me. Playing in front of the so-called chicken run at Upton Park, you knew when you were playing badly, believe me. Invariably I'd turn to Billy Bonds for some kind of moral support. Billy wasn't the most talented player but had the biggest heart and was a huge influence on me. The one thing I learned from Billy was that if you gave 110 per cent every Saturday the fans would be on your side. If you gave 55 per cent they would crucify you. But he wasn't the only one who helped me. Bobby Moore was also a great role model. So, of course, was Geoff, who gave me little tips: how to hold the ball up, how to knock it off, how to spin and go. Martin Peters was the quiet one but prior to his move to Spurs he helped my game, like telling me how to time my runs and not be offside. I always made a point of trying to pick people's brains from different clubs too. Soccer players by nature are not selfish people, not in my day at least. They were willing to share information.

✱

GEOFF AND I WERE CERTAINLY READING EACH OTHER'S GAME WELL and we had the makings of a great partnership. A few weeks after our triumph over Leeds we were scheduled to play a London derby game against Crystal Palace. Geoff was unavailable through injury and I was really pleased to see Ade Coker get a chance in the first team. Ade was born in Lagos, Nigeria, in 1954 and had arrived in London with his family when he was eleven years old. He was a skinny little guy and I had taken him under my wing at Chadwell Heath. He lived in Fulham and had a long journey to training each day. If I remember correctly, he had to take the District Line, or at least start off that way.

Ade was a natural footballer. Everything seemed to come easy to him. I had played with him in the reserves and always marvelled at the way he could take on opponents, spinning 180 degrees and leaving them for dead. It was a treat just watching him. Needless to say, he played a major role in our victory that day against Palace. With only five minutes on the clock, Harry Redknapp flung over a corner which the Palace defence could only half-clear. The ball went straight to Ade, who lashed a left-foot volley into the back of the net. A header from Billy

Bonds put us two up with only a quarter of an hour played. Try as they might in front of their own supporters, Palace never looked like getting back into it and it was all over when I cracked in a third twenty minutes from time to give us a 3–0 victory, sending our travelling fans off to the local tube station in excellent voice and heart.

The newspapers were full of praise for Ade and rightly so. One headline read 'Coker's Cracker' and another 'EE-AYE-ADE-O!' There was a far more significant factor that bright October afternoon in 1971. It was the first time that two 'coloured' players – as we were known then – had played together in West Ham's first team. While it was a wonderful statement about the ability of non-whites, it also meant more racial abuse, which I had been subjected to often, mostly in the north of England.

After the Second World War immigration to the UK took off big time from countries like India and Pakistan (which had just gained independence), and Jamaica and Barbados (which would follow suit in the 1960s). Many of them settled in the East End of London, which became a melting pot for Jewish, Irish and Eastern European immigrants as well as those from ex-colonial countries. Football, however, was still very much a white man's sport, but West Ham was an obvious place for young aspiring black players to gravitate towards.

I wish it had been the same all over the country. It wasn't. Every time you played an away game it was a challenge. I kind of built myself up for it ahead of time and just tried to ignore it. It's easy to react to monkey chants and bananas being thrown at you, but are you reacting for the right reasons? Don't forget, we were often playing in front of 50,000 or 60,000 fans and I was the only player people would pick on. I knew exactly who they were targeting.

The south of the country was slightly more cosmopolitan and tolerant. It was always the teams up north that were the worst offenders – like Leeds, for instance. I really don't know why, it's just the way it was. You had to accept it. You had to have a thick skin. Otherwise I think I would have cracked. I remember Brendan Batson as a young boy at Arsenal not really getting a chance. The coaching staff at Highbury perhaps didn't fancy him. Arsenal had a double-winning team at the time so I can't say whether being black gave him fewer opportunities. I know Sol Campbell says black players were still being treated differently when he played three decades later.

All I can say from my time at West Ham is that Ron Greenwood didn't treat me any differently. In fact, he was the first coach to give us black players an opportunity to showcase our talent. A few years later, although he didn't play for West Ham, I remember seeing Laurie Cunningham as a young boy. I knew straight away he'd be a household name. He was nicknamed the Black Flash – for obvious reasons. The boy was blessed with breathtaking ability. I wonder what he'd be worth today.

I've heard people say that West Ham fans also used to get on my back. I wasn't really aware of it at the time but if that's true it was only a minority, perhaps members of the National Front, which targeted football games to re-cruit new members in the 1970s and 80s. Maybe there were a few who couldn't accept West Ham having a black player but they were never really vocal – unlike fans of Leeds, Everton and others. I lost count of the number of monkey chants directed at me. It didn't help that there were characters like Alf Garnett on the popular television show, *Till Death Us Do Part*, who quite openly referred to black people as 'coons'. In those days there was no such thing as political cor-rectness. *Till Death Us Do Part* regularly attracted audiences of several million every week. I can't help but think the programme, even though it was supposed to be satirical, helped to give licence to people to mimic his name-calling. The character was West Ham through and through, but I'm not sure he portrayed an accurate image of the average Hammer. What was laughable for some people, others might have been offended by.

Under Ron Greenwood's leadership, skin colour had no relationship to skill or ability. Ron used to say to me, 'When you hear all those remarks, first of all ignore them. Second, stick the ball in the net. That will shut them up.' He was correct and that's exactly what I always tried to do. The problem never really went away, but that is how I dealt with it and I always received 100 per cent support from the rest of my team-mates as well as our wonderful supporters.

And yet, depressingly, racism still rears its ugly head today – and not just among the fans. In 2011, two generations on from the abuse I used to get from the terraces, Luis Suarez, playing for Liverpool at the time, infamously used the most disgraceful racist language towards Patrice Evra. I think he should have been banned from football. Did he not realise that he was supposed to be a role model as well for young fans? After that incident, CNN sent a television crew to Bermuda to interview me. I told them what Ron Greenwood always said. 'The football doesn't care what colour you are. Give your answer by sticking one in the back of the net.'

If I am not mistaken, Suarez argued that where he comes from, Uruguay, the kind of language he used was not really considered unacceptable. That's a spurious argument. But Suarez wasn't the only player to prove that, much as we'd like to think we've got rid of racism, there is still a nasty undercurrent, even if incidents are thankfully few and far between nowadays. The John Terry case involving Anton Ferdinand was a case in point. What I've always said is that people have to look at themselves in the mirror and the authorities simply have to take firmer action. How many games did Suarez and Terry get banned for? Eight and four respectively. Not enough in my opinion. The FA and Premier League must show once and for all that racism in all forms cannot be tolerated. I don't actually think Terry has much to complain about in terms of the judgement.

Let's face it, in 2016 people were still talking about racism in the same way as when I played. These things should be long sorted out by now. The game doesn't belong to one colour or one race of people. It belongs to everyone. That's why Pelé called it the beautiful game. What's the first thing that happens when a goal is scored? Everyone gets hugged. People don't look at your colour then, do they?

Football is an international game. The Premier League is televised on all six continents. Young children of every race, colour and creed, rich and poor, worship the heroes they see playing every week. For many children in less-developed countries, football is all they have. They expect their heroes to play and behave like heroes – with dignity. Perhaps that is why I was successful in England when other black players of the time struggled. I did not see myself as any kind of pioneer, I just tried to behave in the best way I could.

11

THRASHING LAW, CHARLTON AND THE 'OTHER' BEST

NOBODY DESERVED A TESTIMONIAL MORE THAN GEOFF HURST and it took place in November 1971. Normally testimonials were against a rival team but the opposition invited by the club to celebrate Geoff's was a select European XI managed by Tommy Docherty. I had to rub my eyes when I watched them all arrive at Upton Park. Virtually every one was a superstar in his own right. There was the great Eusebio (Portugal), Uwe Seeler – Germany's centre-forward in 1966 – Dave Mackay (Spurs), Tommy Gemmell (Celtic) and Rodney Marsh (QPR) to name but five.

What a grand evening it was. We shared eight goals in front of a huge crowd as the fans roared their appreciation of all the marvellous talent assembled to celebrate the unique occasion. Guess how much the fans paid to watch the game that evening? Well, to sit in the East Stand cost exactly £1, as did blocks B, C and D of the West Stand. Entry to A and E blocks in the West Stand was 75p. Those in the East and West Enclosures paid 50p for the privilege, while those who watched from the North and South Banks were charged 40p. Children under the age of fourteen got into the ground for 20p. I shake my head sometimes when I see what supporters have to pay these days to go and watch a football match. In my playing days it was truly a working man's sport, and many men still worked on the docks on Saturday morning then went to the pub for a pint before coming to home games.

After the testimonial we all went to a local club for a reception and watched as Geoff cut his celebration cake. Typical of the man, he took the cake to a London hospital where it was shared with nurses and staff.

It's a sign of the times that testimonials are rapidly becoming a thing of the past. Why is that? Perhaps because one-club men are a dying breed. Money controls football today so it doesn't surprise me that players don't tend to stay very long at one club and go where the money is. Some players are only in it to see how much money they can get, and some contracts are not worth the paper they are written on because they can be ripped up at any time. It would be nice if we could get back to the days when fans could say, 'Hey, that guy played for so-and-so for all those years.' But I suppose if you are being paid £300,000 a week, do you really need a testimonial?

I guess I'm old-fashioned. When I was a player most of my contemporaries had a true affection for a particular club. I'm not sure that's the case any longer. It was good for the fans because they could identify with the team. Nowadays it seems some players are happy just to sit on the bench and take the money. I would have much preferred to be playing week in, week out. You don't improve while sitting on the bench collecting your wages, that I can definitely tell you. To my mind, you improve by being on the field every Saturday for ninety minutes. You owe it not only to yourself but also to the fans.

THE 1971/72 SEASON WAS PICKING UP AND INJURIES WERE FEW, but our league form was nothing for me to write home to Bermuda about. We suffered home defeats against Sheffield United and Manchester City, although I managed to snatch one of the goals in a 3–3 away draw at Southampton and was particularly pleased when I opened one of the London newspapers and saw my name in the list of top scorers in the First Division at the beginning of December (the League Cup totals are in brackets):

Martin Chivers (Spurs)	14 (5)	19
Francis Lee (Man City)	18 (1)	19
George Best (Man United)	14 (3)	17

Alan Woodward (Sheffield United)	12 (5)	17
Malcolm Macdonald (Newcastle United)	14 (1)	15
Clyde Best (West Ham)	10 (4)	14

This was definitely one of the clippings that I posted to my family back home. Christmas was coming again but once more there could be little thought of relaxation or having a 'knees-up' down the pub. We had a game at Spurs on Boxing Day, which fell on Monday 27 December that year, and we had not won a league match, home or away, for seven games.

Thankfully, we were at least given Christmas Day off training at Chadwell Heath to be with our friends and families, but we were very much focused on improving our form and certainly didn't want to make it eight disappointing results in a row. I spent Christmas Day quietly. I called the family in Bermuda, had Christmas dinner with the Charles family and watched Her Majesty the Queen's Christmas message on television – just as we all still do today. Sometimes, I admit, I got homesick. I never quite got used to it being pitch-black by about 4 p.m. My thoughts used to turn to home where the sun sets gently in a golden ball over the Atlantic, even on short December days, and the rays cast beautiful shadows over the white roofs of our houses before fading into evening.

When I looked out of the windows of our team bus en route to north London on the Monday, I could see the moon quite clearly. London derbies are something special. They become the 'topic of the week' for everyone, starting from the final whistle of the previous game. There is no need for fans to travel long distances by coach or train: every stadium is just a short tube or bus ride away.

When we arrived at White Hart Lane the ground was rapidly filling up, with long lines outside the turnstiles even though there was still two hours to go before kick-off. In those days there were no all-seater stadiums and there were 54,000 people crammed into the ground. Spurs had been unbeaten in their last seven games and came at us like a tidal wave but we stood firm. Our defence would not allow Martin Chivers or Alan Gilzean, Tottenham's demon duo up front, a sniff of the ball. Their best opportunities in the first half were created by their centre-half Mike England coming up for corner kicks. I used to think that with a name like that, Mike had to be English. Actually, he was Wales through and through. We kept a clean sheet until half-time and sensed that we could get something from the game.

Our chance came just after the ref blew his whistle to start the second half. Trevor Brooking swung over a corner and although Ray Evans was marking me, I managed to get my head on it and nodded it in at the near post. That goal galvanised Spurs into attack after frantic attack. We were even able to hear the roars from outside the ground where thousands had been locked out. We held on to our narrow lead for the remainder of the game and took the applause of our supporters as we ran up the tunnel.

It is difficult to explain the culture of British football to those who have never experienced it, especially if you live in North America where I spent a lot of my career and where stadiums are often purpose-built and situated away from inner-city conurbations.

Football is a religion in England. Kickabouts can take place just about anywhere, in a nondescript field next to a factory or any local park. When the professional game in England was developing, most people lived near their place of work. It meant that the churches, tobacconists, pubs, newsagents, fish 'n' chip shops and football grounds all grew up cheek by jowl with each other.

It is still like that to a certain extent at some clubs, although many of the old tenement buildings have been demolished. I always enjoyed waving to our fans from the team bus as they made their way to their favourite pubs and cafés near our ground. It was quite common for fans to come home from work on a Saturday lunchtime, go to the pub for a pint, nip next door to the bookie's to place a bet, then walk across the street to watch their favourite team play – never having travelled more than a few hundred yards.

There was little thought of relaxation during the lead-up to New Year's Day, especially with the mighty Manchester United about to occupy the away changing room at the Boleyn Ground. We were all walking on air after that win against Spurs – but I secretly knew that some of the lads did 'relax' a bit in the run-up to New Year's Eve, if you get my drift. Not this 'Bermuda Bye from Somerset', though. No chance.

My brother Carlton was doing a telecommunications course in Norwood, not far from Crystal Palace in southwest London, and I caught the train over to see him. It was lovely being with him at this time of year. Remember, I was still only twenty and, even though Mrs Charles treated me like one of her own, there was still that occasional yearning for everything Bermudian over the Christmas holiday – the cassava pie, macaroni cheese dishes, peas 'n' rice at all the 'open house' events in the neighbourhood, and the Christmas lights on our palmetto palm trees in the garden.

On New Year's Eve, Mrs Charles had our favourite meal ready – roast beef, Yorkshire puddings and mashed potatoes (of course!) – but that was the sum total of our partying. While Londoners splashed in the fountains of Trafalgar Square as Big Ben chimed in the New Year, the Hammer from Bermuda was tucked up, sound asleep upstairs at 23 Ronald Avenue, getting ready to play the Red Devils the next day.

I reported to the ground just after lunchtime and watched as the West Ham supporters, many of them no doubt hung over from the night before, passed through the turnstiles to get the best vantage points from the terraces. The club had warned them to get there early because they knew we would have a capacity crowd.

By 2 p.m. the pubs were already emptying and hastily drained pint glasses lined the counters. I felt sorry for the United fans. They would have had to have been on their way down south from the crack of dawn, completing what would be a 400-mile round trip by the time they got home – and they were not even guaranteed entry.

It was freezing cold with slate-grey skies – what else? – and the floodlights at Upton Park had been switched on as early as 1 p.m. to lighten the gloom. Sir Matt Busby had retired from his second stint as United boss at the end of the previous season and Frank O'Farrell had taken his place.

The gates were locked about fifteen minutes before kick-off with 42,000 in the ground and many United fans left outside. They must have felt so frustrated. These days if you can't get in or you're late for the game, you can go round the corner and watch on Sky or BT Sport if the action is being televised live. There was no such technology as satellite television or cable TV back then. The only way of tuning in would be if the match was being broadcast over the radio. Otherwise it was a question of watching highlights later on – and even then only if your match was one of the few chosen.

Top of the league, United had lost just two of their first 23 fixtures and had accumulated 35 points (remember, it was one point for a draw and two points for a win), while we were in twelfth place. The television cameras were also at the stadium so that highlights (for those poor United fans locked out) could be shown that evening. Actually there was one camera, situated in the stand. Nowadays there are cameras on the touchline, cameras behind the goals, mobile cameras etc., all giving instant replays from different angles. That one television camera in the stand had to cover the entire game!

And what a game it was.

Teams such as Manchester United don't sit back and defend when they play away games. It is not in their nature. Their worldwide following demands entertainment and attacking football and that is what the Red Devils have provided down the years, with the exception of the occasional bland era. Reputations count for nothing at Old Trafford if you don't do things in style. For all the trophies he had won at his previous clubs, for all his stature as one of the best in the business, Louis van Gaal quickly discovered this when he took over from David Moyes.

The United that came to the Boleyn ground on the first day of 1972 had bags of style – and a whole lot more. Not least, three of the most famous names in twentieth-century football – Denis Law, George Best and Bobby Charlton.

But we refused to be intimidated by them, not after our fabulous result against Spurs. Play raged from end to end, with neither side giving the other an inch. Our hearts were in our mouths for the first half-hour as first Frank Lampard then Billy Bonds made a couple of desperate goal-line clearances from Law and Charlton. Then we struck five minutes before half-time courtesy of Pop Robson's audacious back-heel – something fairly unique at the time. I think they must have heard the roar throughout the whole of the East End and it got better still. The second half was only five minutes old when I got my head on a Trevor Brooking cross to score. United did not lie down. They never did. They came tearing at us. George Best hit the post before Charlton rattled our crossbar with a tremendous volley. Five minutes before the final whistle, however, we could breathe more easily. Geoff Hurst was needlessly pulled down in the United penalty box and converted the penalty himself.

Not only the London tabloids but all the national newspapers were glowing in their praise for both sides. *The Times* noted: 'It was one of those afternoons when you had to hug yourself at the end of it and bless your good fortune that you were there on the day that West Ham United and Manchester United produced a game of breathtaking skill and invention. United found the Hammers producing their best form for a long while.'

To say that we were thrilled with our performances over the holiday period is an understatement. We had stopped a miserable run of draws and defeats and given ourselves a massive morale boost for the second half of the season after taking maximum points from games against two of the strongest teams in the league.

After we had showered and changed, both teams met in the players' lounge for a beer. The Manchester lads took defeat graciously and we in turn agreed that it could have turned out differently if some of those United misses had gone in. However, that's football.

We all shook hands and went our separate ways, though I have to say Messrs Law, Best and Charlton, together with the rest of them, were not in a particularly cheery mood as they trooped towards their team bus. If someone with a crystal ball had told me that within two years the mighty Red Devils, the famous Manchester United, would be relegated, I would have laughed my head off and accused the person of having drunk too much pale ale. But that's exactly what happened in 1974, by which time Best, Law and Charlton had left.

Before I forget, let me right now pay tribute to the Band of the Royal British Legion that played at our home games. Nowadays there are all sorts of digital and computerised musical performances which can be downloaded and sent through state-of-the-art stadium sound systems at an ear-splitting volume. Well, we didn't have anything like that. We had something better. The British Legion Band provided a terrific medley of military-style songs both before the game and at half-time. God bless all of its members. They turned up in their uniforms, regardless of the weather, often in pouring rain or sleet. I used to wonder how they could play their tubas when their fingers were frozen stiff.

I got home late to my digs and Mrs Charles had the usual fare all ready for me. You know what it is by now! On the television there was talk of some kind of industrial action on the way from the coalminers' union but I hardly paid any attention. I had played really well and scored in both of the holiday fixtures, receiving the applause of a packed Boleyn Ground. You can't get much better than that. I had a three-bar electric heater in my room and I turned it up full to warm up the place. Before I went to sleep I wondered how everyone was back home in Bermuda – and made a mental note to call a certain young lady in Somerset.

Her name was Alfreida Swan.

12

SO CLOSE TO WEMBLEY, YET SO FAR

JANUARY AND FEBRUARY WERE SHAPING UP AS REALLY BUSY months, especially since we were in the latter stages of the League Cup. After that amazing game at Leeds in October we had gone on to defeat Liverpool at home 2–1 in the fourth round before demolishing Sheffield United 5–0 in the fifth (I grabbed a brace while Pop Robson smashed in a hat-trick).

Beating Sheffield United was another particularly poignant evening for me because in the main stand watching were three of Bermuda's senior politicians: government leader Sir Henry Tucker, the member for finance the Hon. Jack Sharpe, and the member for government organisation the Hon. John Plowman. They had been in London on government business and on their return to the island they duly reported that 'Clyde had a great game and we were all very proud of our fellow Bermudian'.

With Wembley within touching distance we were drawn against Stoke City in the two-legged semi-final, which should have been settled before Christmas. We got off on the right foot, beating them 2–1 at their place. It turned out to be a tough, bad-tempered game with four players booked, two from each side. Bobby Moore was one of them when he brought down Jimmy Greenhoff from behind, just inches outside the box. For a split second, our hearts stopped, wondering if it was going to be a penalty. Frank Lampard was also booked for dissent when he started challenging some of the referee's decisions.

Peter Dobing had given Stoke the lead but Billy Bonds was working his magic with his through balls from midfield. During one attack on the Stoke goal I was sent flying by Dobing, and ended up sprawled on the turf inside the area. Geoff Hurst stepped up calmly and took the spot kick, sending it flying past Gordon Banks.

In the second half, Billy's through-ball found Harry Redknapp on the wing. Harry crossed to me and I just hit it first time. Gordon Banks said later that it was one of the best goals he had ever conceded. We held on for a fine 2–1 win and were favourites to go through to the final.

But it didn't quite pan out that way. We lost 0–1 at home for a 2-2 aggregate score, with Hursty this time missing a penalty that Banks miraculously managed to tip over the bar. It meant that we needed a replay at a neutral ground – Hillsborough, home of Sheffield Wednesday. It also meant another long trip for our supporters in early January, not all of whom could make it, and we were grateful that the majority of the few thousand local Wednesday fans who attended the game were on our side. Neither team could make the breakthrough, so now we were now looking at a second replay. Once again we drew the short straw as far as distance was concerned, and we groaned in collective dismay as Old Trafford was chosen. I was getting a bit tired of platform 13 at Euston station!

Not only that, but it would be another midweek game. It meant that our fans had to get off work by midday to catch the train to Manchester's Piccadilly – and then get buses from there to Old Trafford. The special 'supporters' trains departed on Wednesday 26 January at 2.40 p.m., arriving in Manchester three hours later. After the game the fans had to get back to Piccadilly station for the journey south, many not getting home until about 1 a.m. The train journey cost £2, while Lacey's Coaches were a bit less at £1.70. At least Lacey's got the fans back all the way to the East End. After all these years, I still salute our fans – the best in the world.

The pitch was terrible and everyone was slipping and sliding all over the place. Our keeper Bobby Ferguson had to go off injured and Bobby Moore had to temporarily take over in goal. He had actually asked me if I wanted to take over, since I had sort of been regarded as a kind of back-up goalie. I had often messed around in training in goal if I wanted to take a breather and I would go between the sticks for real on one occasion against Leeds in April 1973 when Bobby Ferguson collided with our own player, John McDowell. We drew the game 1–1 and I thought I should have done better when Allan 'Sniffer' Clarke scored. One or two newspaper reports suggested Ron Greenwood had wanted to hand the jersey to Trevor Brooking but chose me because Trevor was causing the Leeds defence problems. He apparently consulted Bobby Moore and it was decided to put me in goal. One report the next day said that the 'giant Bermudan wowed the fans with a classic right-fist punch' from a Mick Jones header. That was the good news. The bad news was what happened in Leeds' next move, the same paper reporting that I was left 'flat-footed' when Clarke scored in the 84th minute 'past a groping Best'. Sounds about right! Still, I don't think I let the team down overall.

Back to 1972, and Bobby wanted me to also go in goal against Stoke, but I was too nervous and declined. Besides, I desperately wanted to score. I remember looking round the ground at the sea of claret and blue scarves and thinking, 'How on earth did so many of them get here in time?' British Rail had filled five and a half trains and later wrote to the club commending the impeccable behaviour of our fans during both parts of the journey.

Of all the Stoke players who opposed us in what was an extraordinary semi-final, no one impressed me more than Jimmy Greenhoff. Jimmy was a fantastic player yet somehow never played for the full England team. Maybe that was because during that period, it seemed as if England had tons and tons of great players. It was such a privilege to play against them. Each team must have had four or five stars who could have played for the national team and never got a chance. Jimmy was one of them. Anyway, after a breathless 420 minutes of football, an epic tie finally reached its extraordinary denouement, but not before Bobby showed a disbelieving crowd that he'd learned a thing or two from Banksy. In keeping with an extraordinary match, Bobby, who temporarily assumed the green jersey for twenty minutes of the first half while keeper Bobby Ferguson received treatment, saved Mike Bernard's spot kick before helplessly watching the same player tuck home the rebound. With almost 50,000 crammed into the ground – it could have been more were it not for the ongoing construction of one of the stands – it was the final act of a compelling drama which, arguably, represented the finest domestic cup semi-final ever played on these shores.

Bobby's heroics while Ferguson received treatment kept us in it and the magnificent Billy Bonds equalised from a heavily deflected shot. Then, with

Bobby Ferguson restored, Trevor Brooking volleyed us in front from Bondsy's cross. Stoke were no pushovers, however. Deep, deep into first half injury time the veteran George Eastham played in Peter Dobing who put Stoke in front. Shortly after the interval Terry Conroy's shot through the mud gave them the advantage. We battled like crazy, but it was not enough. Stoke had edged us 3–2 in front of a packed house.

We were heartbroken and left Old Trafford with tears as well as the driving rain running down our faces. This is not poetic licence. We were really crying. Many of us were 21 or 22 and to get to a semi-final was a massive step. Getting beaten in the way we did was really painful.

WE WERE OUT OF THE LEAGUE CUP BUT IT WAS JANUARY – AND January is FA Cup third-round month in England, always has been. Third-round day is when the big boys from the two top divisions come in. In my day, the third-round draw was enormous, something you always looked forward to. It's one of the great traditions. Even if you were in the treatment room, the trainers would have the radio on to find out who we were playing. It was always a magical time, lunchtime on a Monday, though sadly nowadays the draw is invariably at the end of the weekend or even on a Monday night. I still love the FA Cup. To me it still ranks as the most prestigious domestic competition in world football.

When we were looking at results from the earlier rounds we noticed a team called Hereford United were doing well. They were a Southern League side and had beaten King's Lynn and Northampton Town to proceed to the third round of the competition against Newcastle. This was all part of what made the competition great – the 'minnows' getting the chance to play a game against the 'big boys' of the top two divisions before inevitably exiting the competition.

Like a lot of my mates at West Ham, I wasn't even sure where Hereford was. Nor did I know the names of the other teams playing in the Southern League. Like a lot of other people in the UK, I was about to find out.

When the draw for the third round was made, we were given a home game against 'The Hatters' – Luton Town from the Second Division. On paper it should have been a cakewalk. It was anything but, a typical cup tie in which we both went at each other from the whistle. Geoff Hurst (who else?) opened the scoring after only two minutes and I tucked one away twenty minutes later. Luton clawed one back in the second half and gave everything they could, but everyone agreed that we were the better team. One Sunday newspaper noted 'either side could have had three or four goals but anything other than a West Ham win would have been unrepresentative'.

The only unhappy moment of that game was the sight of Bobby Moore being stretchered off after just five minutes. I had never seen him injured before and we all watched anxiously as he was carried up the tunnel. Fortunately, X-rays showed that he had received nothing more serious than a blow on the nerve in his ankle and he was able to return to the ground that evening. We were all really relieved.

After the game we sat in the home changing room and watched the rest of the cup results come in on television. We noticed that the Newcastle vs Hereford game had been postponed because of heavy rain. In fact, the weather was so bad that the game was actually postponed twice and was not played until 24 January, by which time we knew that we would be playing the eventual winner – which we naturally assumed would be Newcastle. Instead, the 39,000 spectators at St James' Park, including 5,000 who had travelled from little Hereford, saw the non-league team hold the mighty Magpies to a 2–2 draw.

The replay in Hereford was also postponed and was eventually played on 5 February, the day allocated for the fourth-round ties. Hereford's ground, Edgar Street, was heaving, with fans even clutching the branches of trees outside the ground. Their heroes were by no means overawed by their illustrious visitors and gave as good as they got. But with just eight minutes left on the clock, United's pressure finally paid off as Malcolm Macdonald nodded home a Viv Busby cross.

Most of those watching assumed that was that. How wrong they were.

With time running out, Ronnie Radford, with a precise piece of opportunism, let fly from thirty yards and saw the ball sail into the top corner of the Newcastle net, immediately turning him into one of the great folk heroes of all time and sparking a pitch invasion. Extra time.

With Newcastle shellshocked, Hereford substitute Ricky George hit a crisp shot past Scotland defender Bobby Moncur and goalie Willie McFaul for the most dramatic of winners, prompting total bedlam and another pitch invasion. The BBC had planned to show only a small clip of the match, with its main 'features' being the fourth-round ties between Liverpool and Leeds United and Preston North End and Manchester United, but because of such a seismic shock, plans were switched at the last minute. For many years since, footage of Hereford's equaliser against Newcastle was part of the *Match of the Day* opening sequence: and right up to the present day the giant-killing of all giant-killings is whispered in every boardroom of every wannabe non-league club.

Like everyone else at West Ham and across the country I could only stand and gaze in astonishment at the incredible scenes in the aftermath of Hereford's victory and it suddenly dawned on all of us that we had to go down there a few days later to take them on. Much has been made of the famous Hereford–Newcastle clash but little of how West Ham were in danger of becoming the next victims of a giant-killing.

The fact is that lightning rarely strikes twice in the FA Cup. Edgar Street was packed to capacity once again, and Hereford came at us with bags of spirit. But we were determined not to go the same way as Newcastle and, though we should have won the game, we had to settle in the end for a draw.

The replay took place on a Monday with a highly unusual 2.15 p.m. kick-off ordered by the FA because of power blackouts and industrial action sweeping the country at the time. Much of UK was on a three-day week, which disturbed a lot of people in England and was something of a novelty to me, even though I respected those who were fighting for what they believed was right. One thing it didn't do was stop our fans from attending in their masses. I don't think anything in England can stop fans going to games, it's in the genes! Look at the cost today compared to when I played, yet still the grounds are full.

Unfortunately, those Hereford fans who came by car misjudged the amount of travelling time necessary to get to east London. To further confuse matters, because of the industrial action, some of the traffic lights were not working and the journey was complicated by extensive roadworks into the capital.

As it turned out, *fifteen* coaches full of Hereford supporters only arrived at Upton Park half an hour after kick-off. In the end we had 42,271 people inside and a hat-trick from Geoff Hurst ensured there would be no upset, even if the visitors did score a consolation goal minutes from time.

When the final whistle blew, Bobby Moore lined us up at the tunnel entrance and we and all the West Ham fans gave a massive round of applause to the Hereford players as they walked off with their heads held high. It was no more than they deserved.

We now looked forward eagerly to visiting our fifth-round opponents, Huddersfield Town. By coincidence, our game against them came exactly one month after Stoke had knocked us out of the League Cup. The omens looked good. We really wanted to get our hands on some silverware and we were very optimistic that we could get a positive result against a side that had failed to score in any of their previous five home league games, giving us a distinct psychological edge.

The game sticks in my mind because 48 hours previously I had attained something of a personal milestone by reaching my 21st birthday. I didn't make a big thing about it at all. There were too many important issues to concern me. Besides, I was still the new kid on the block playing alongside men whose faces and names were recognised throughout the international football world.

Still, it gave me that extra bit of confidence and enthusiasm to have turned 21 and I looked forward to celebrating it by knocking Huddersfield out of the FA Cup. Wishful thinking. By the time the ref blew for full time we were on the end of a 4–2 defeat that wrecked our Wembley hopes for another season.

They carved open our defence after 23 minutes for their opening goal, although Pop Robson equalised for us on the stroke of half-time. In the second half they ripped us apart, scoring in the 51st, 68th and 70th minutes. I duly got the goal to mark my birthday, but it was all about the team.

Our lack of consistency often made me really frustrated. It's annoying when you know you have supremely talented players but you are not where you want to be. What has often hurt us at West Ham is that we've always wanted to play the game the right way. But playing 'nice' football, especially in the years I played, was not always going to yield results. What was it Jack Charlton used to say? 'When in doubt, lash it out.' But we would probably have put it differently: 'play it out'. At times you could say that was perhaps our Achilles heel, but if you ask Hammers fans of any era, most would probably tell you that's one of the reasons they support the club.

You could have heard a pin drop on the train journey back. We seemed to be caught up in the general wave of despair gripping the country, manifested in all kinds of other ways. For example, the previous week our Supporters Association had to cancel their annual dance that was to have taken place at Stratford Town Hall – because of the power cuts.

13

WEST HAM'S OWN THREE DEGREES

THE WEEK AFTER HUDDERSFIELD PUT US OUT OF THE CUP WE gained our revenge with a 3–0 league win at Upton Park when I bagged another brace. Our form was erratic, there was no doubt about that. But we had some tremendously talented players in our first team and received many complimentary remarks from sports writers in the London and national press about the attractive way we played.

Strangely enough, we seemed to do better against teams at the top of the table compared to those below. A few days before our final epic struggle with Stoke in the League Cup, Brian Clough brought his Derby County team to Upton Park. Practically the whole side had either international experience or bags of ability – or both: Colin Boulton, Ron Webster, John Robson, Colin Todd, Roy McFarland, John McGovern, Archie Gemmill, Kevin Hector, Alan Hinton and John O'Hare. It was an absolute classic as we shared six goals, both teams leaving the pitch to applause – even from the press.

That Derby team would end up winning the league that year whereas we could never maintain that kind of momentum. We lost narrowly away to teams such as Wolves and Ipswich Town when we should have done a lot better. Because of fixture congestion due to bad winter weather we had to play back-to-back home games – and I mean back to back. In other words, with not a single day's gap. Can you imagine any team in any division being asked today to play 24 hours after the other? Yet that is exactly what we had to do on 31 March and

1 April 1972, against first Leeds and then Spurs the very next day.

Like the rest of the team, I was feeling the effects of a long, hard league and cup campaign. We were all knackered, with the usual round of injuries that besets every team. Though I must say, in my case I was incredibly lucky with injuries compared to my peers. Maybe it had something to do with my size, I'm not sure. But the fact is I played almost every season injury-free.

Friday 31 March 1972 was Good Friday, a public holiday in Bermuda just as it was in the UK and elsewhere – but with a difference. On Good Friday back home the custom has always been to have family kite-flying celebrations and to bake fishcakes, which we put on hot cross buns. The whole island comes to a halt. Schoolchildren have kite competitions in the run-up to the holiday in which prizes are awarded for best design, most colourful kite, first kite to fly above a certain height and so on.

The tradition has been in existence for ages – no one knows quite how long. One fable often repeated is that it began with a Sunday school teacher's creative lesson on Jesus Christ's ascension to heaven. It is said that the teacher made a cross kite, took it to a hilltop and set it flying, then cut the string and the students watched it sail upwards towards heaven. I'm not sure if that's entirely true, but Good Friday is always avidly awaited. The sky is transformed into a dancing mosaic of brilliant and beautiful shapes, colours and sounds, interrupted only by the temptation of those fishcakes – made of cod and potatoes, deep-fried with onions and parsley – and those delicious hot cross buns. In the old days, people who made the kites spent months preparing them, carefully crafted from colourful tissue paper and clear white pine wood. Great care was taken to ensure that the colours blended perfectly. Some of us still make our own but unfortunately today's busy lifestyle leaves little time for such pastimes. Imported plastic kites are becoming popular because of their convenience and lower price.

On this Good Friday Leeds were top of the table at the time, while we were twelfth, and they brought their talent-filled team to the Boleyn Ground. The press box was almost overflowing, not least because there was only one other top-flight game taking place that day. Leeds were challenging Derby County, Manchester City and Arsenal every step of the way for the title; they were all within a point of each other and everyone was keen to find out if West Ham could knock Leeds out of their stride.

We pummelled them in the first half, with Billy Bonds opening the scoring and Geoff Hurst adding a second on the half-hour. We looked as if we could add to that after the interval but Leeds came roaring back, even though they were without the injured Mick Jones and Johnny Giles. Eddie Gray scored a couple of scorchers not long after half-time to level matters and that's the way it finished, which was probably a fair result.

Amazingly, as I've said, we had to play again 24 hours later on Easter Saturday, but it turned out to be one of my most memorable games for West Ham – the latest of many battles with Tottenham Hotspur. In terms of career milestones, 1 April 1972 has to go down as a special landmark when Ron Greenwood became the first manager to select not one, not two, but three black players in the same league game: Clive Charles, Ade Coker and myself all lined up in a 2–0 victory at Upton Park. It was April Fools' Day and the cynics no doubt questioned whether we were really playing or had just been sent out to warm up.

Ron was a pioneer in every sense of the word and later selected Viv Anderson as the first black player ever to appear for England. For all the recognition of Greenwood as a great coach and motivator, he struck an equally telling blow to those who thought the colour of our skin was an impediment to our ability to play.

Perhaps I also saw something of myself in Ade. Here he was, aged seventeen, playing in a massive London derby, feeling extremely nervous and being coached and helped by an old . . . well, a twenty-year-old . . . team-mate. Ade, who got the second against Spurs, ended up only making eleven senior appearances for us and disappeared from the spotlight almost as soon as he had arrived. It's only my opinion, but the size of Ade perhaps had something to do with that. He had great touch but in those days most of us strikers were big guys and perhaps his smaller stature hindered him. Had he played on the Continent, where power was not such a prerequisite, he may have become a household name. He eventually excelled in the NASL, and represented the USA during the qualifying round for the 1986 World Cup, having taken US citizenship.

We didn't really look at it as three black players in an otherwise white team. It was more a case of, hey, we're all mates together. I think most English clubs back then were naive and scared to give black players a chance. Some of the best players in the world – like Pelé and Eusebio – were black but in England we didn't get the same opportunities as we do now. Black players have almost always had rhythm and movement but very few were given the credit for that when I first arrived from Bermuda. A competitor should always be judged on ability.

One other thing about that Spurs game I'd like to point out. Once Kevin Lock came on as a sub (he set up Ade's goal with Trevor Brooking netting the other), the average age of our side was reduced to 21, which made our performance all the more unbelievable. Bill Nicholson couldn't believe that players so young could knock the ball around so well – ironically, rather like the modern Spurs team under Mauricio Pochettino. Tottenham were also regarded as a footballing side but we beat them at their own game that day – much to the delight of our supporters.

West Ham fans have always had a strong rivalry with Spurs. They are the side the fans always loved us to beat, even if perhaps it's not the same the other way round because Spurs supporters consider Arsenal and Chelsea far more prized scalps. For the players and coaching staff, however, even though there was competition on the field, both teams got on really well with each other and it was great to hear a manager with the reputation of Bill Nick say such nice things about us.

Naturally, I shall never forget the game. I felt such pride that I was joined by Clive and Ade. There was additional significance in the result. Spurs were the only team who we were able to do the 'double' over that season. And one more thing: their captain was Martin Peters, who had left us the previous year, a move which, as I have previously chronicled, infuriated our fans.

Strangely, the fact that there were three black guys in the team for the first time did not even make the newspapers, although Jimmy Hill did make mention of it on *Match of the Day*. That was really heart-warming. I only ever met Jimmy once but I knew that he and Ron Greenwood were good friends. All of us footballers have to be thankful to Jimmy over how he fought for our wages when he was president of the PFA and successfully campaigned for an end to the maximum wage. When you look and see what players earn today compared to his day and mine, you realise what a debt we owed Jimmy. Wages would not have spiralled as they have over the last half-century if Jimmy hadn't gone to war on behalf of the players.

The week before the Spurs game, two of our players had competed in the London Professional Footballers' Athletic Championships at the Crystal Palace

Sports Arena, a track and field meet for players based in the capital, sponsored by the *Evening Standard* and amazingly well attended. It was a fun event, something different from day-to-day training. Bobby Ferguson and Clive Charles both distinguished themselves: Bobby won the 100 metres in 11.3 seconds to retain his title and Clive won the 400 metres in 53.4 seconds. I was reminded of this, two generations later, when I was watching the Olympic track events at London 2012.

IF THE SPURS GAME WAS AN ICONIC OCCASION, ANOTHER fixture that stood out in the 1971/72 season was a League Cup tie back in October with Liverpool. I remember the legend that was Bill Shankly arriving in the away changing room with a squad that comprised (including the one substitute you were allowed back then) Ray Clemence, Tommy Smith, Bobby Graham, Alun Evans, Ian Ross, Larry Lloyd, Emlyn Hughes, Chris Lawler, John Toshack, Ian Callaghan and Steve Heighway.

It was a terrific game watched by a crowd of over 40,000 which saw us concede a goal against the run of play in the first half. Geoff Hurst pulled one back for us and 'Pop' Robson got the winner six minutes from time, a header from only a foot away from the goal-line. We were all elated: we had been playing well since our initial hiccup at the beginning of the season and Ron Greenwood was named Manager of the Month for October. Tony Derry, sales manager of Bell's, presented him with a gallon bottle of whisky and a cheque for £100 before the subsequent game with Manchester City in recognition of the Hammers' undefeated record that month. This included five league games and three League Cup ties.

In the evenings I used to sit in my digs with a pair of scissors and a pile of newspapers at my feet, cutting out football reports and stories about West Ham so that I could post them by air mail to my family back home. It's all now in a scrapbook which was compiled with the help of a good friend in Bermuda who followed my career from day one and which I have kept all these years. Diligently collecting all this paperwork may seem incredible to a 21st-century generation brought up with the Internet, mobile phones, iPods, cable television, instant replays and all the other advances in technology which make up the digital age. But in the early 1970s even the humble fax machine had not been developed sufficiently to be used as a communication tool. And there were only three television stations to choose from.

The only method I had of getting in touch with my family was by phone or air mail letter. My name was appearing frequently, not just in the tabloids, but in the broadsheet so-called 'serious' newspapers such as the *Sunday Times*. I was constantly asked for interviews and reporters were always curious about where I came from and what Bermuda was like. When I told them that we had pink bus stops and drove our cars at 20mph they would put their pens down and look at me as if I was having them on.

BOTH CLIVE AND I HAD PASSED OUR DRIVING TESTS BY THIS TIME – I got my licence a few weeks before him – but even before then we scraped up enough money between us to purchase a second-hand Morris Minor from Harry Redknapp's brother-in-law in the hope we would soon be eligible to drive it. I can't remember what it cost but I do know it was too good a deal to turn down, even though we still had to pass our respective tests. You know Harry, the best wheeler-dealer in the business. I loved Harry, a genuine East Ender who would bend over backwards to make sure you were comfortable in every way. We were totally different characters but, when in Rome, as they say. I learned what Harry was about. He epitomised the happy family mentality of the club. I can't recall a single bad word I ever exchanged with him. Clive and I were so proud of that old 'banger'. It wasn't a Ferrari or Lamborghini, the kind of cars you see footballers turning up to training in these days, but at least it started first time – well, most of the time – and ran well. We'd take it in turns to drive to training and back and after games used to jump into it and 'roar' along Green Street, if you can call it that, on the way home to Ronald Avenue. The arrangement worked quite well but in the end we both bought new cars and got rid of it, though I must say I had a special relationship with that car. Remember the type I mean? The indicator arm used to flap out whenever you turned left or right. It certainly served its purpose.

From Bermuda to the Boleyn… That's me second from the left on the back row as an island footballer… And in very different climes in East London. *(Personal collection/ Mirrorpix)*

Scoring my first goal for West Ham against Burnley in October 1969. *(Press Association)*

A cold wake up call in a 4-0 home defeat to Manchester City in December 1969. *(Mirrorpix)*

A proud Hammer. Posing pre-match in March 1970. *(Mirrorpix)*

In action in West Ham's FA Cup tie with Hereford in 1972. *(Getty)*

In full flow in Ronnie Boyce's 1972 testimonial against Manchester United. *(Colorsport)*

On your marks! Preparing for the Soccer Players Athletic meeting at Crystal Palace with my West Ham teammates. *(Mirrorpix)*

On the Upton Park terraces with Geoff Hurst, Harry Redknapp, Trevor Brooking, Pop Robson, Ronnie Boyce and John Ayris. *(Peter Robinson/ Empics/ PA)*

Ready, aim, fire! Going close against Hull City in the 1973 FA Cup. *(Courtesy of Steve Marsh)*

Shoulder to shoulder with Luton Town's Chris Nicholl. *(Press Association)*

In action at Selhurst Park in a 3-0 win over Palace in 1971. *(Mirrorpix)*

A Boleyn scrapbook; scenes from some of the happiest and most eventful years of my life. *(Mirrorpix/ Press Association/ Colorsport)*

Big in America. In action for Portland Timbers (*Press Association*); training for Toronto Blizzard (*Getty*) and with my Blizzard teammates in 1982. *(Courtesy David Fairclough)*

TORONTO BLIZZARD SOCCER CLUB

Front Row--Left to Right: Duncan Davidson #18, Pasquale Deluca #12, David McQueen #28,
Frank Ciaccia #14, Paul James #15, Cliff Calvert #10.
Middle Row--Left to Right: David Turner (Assistant Coach), Jomo Sono #11, Juan Carlos
Molina #21, Sam Lenarduzzi #4, Patrick "Ace" Ntsoelengoe #8, Bob Houghton (Coach),
David Bryne #19, Bruce Wilson #2, Alan Merrick #23, Jim Panno (Equipment Manager).
Third Row--Left to Right: Gary Kraft #30, David Needham #26, Neill Roberts #6,
Clyde Best #17, Jan Moller #00, Victor Kodelja #7, David Fairclough #20, Randy Ragan #16,
Tony Chursky #1.

I was very proud to receive my MBE in the January 2006 New Years Honours list. *(Personal collection)*

THE ACID TEST

*

RON GREENWOOD KEPT FAITH IN HIS YOUNG PROTÉGÉS WHEN we went to Highbury near the end of the season. In addition to Kevin Lock, Clive Charles and Ade Coker we also had nineteen-year-old Joe Durrell, an East End youngster from Stepney who had been doing well in the Football Combination. On paper it was a relatively meaningless end-of-season game. However, there was still something at stake. The game would decide the season's unofficial 'London Championship', which is based upon results of top-flight games between clubs in the capital. It was a far bigger deal in my day than now and we were disappointed, therefore, to lose by the odd goal in three against the Gunners, Trevor Brooking equalising with a cracker of a volley either side of two Alan Ball goals. Here's how the 'London Championship' finished that season:

	P	W	D	L	F	A	Pts
Arsenal	8	4	4	0	12	6	12
West Ham United	8	4	2	2	11	7	10
Chelsea	8	4	0	4	11	14	8
Tottenham Hotspur	8	2	3	3	8	6	7
Crystal Palace	8	0	3	5	8	17	3

That unofficial London table aside, the 1971/72 season had been a pretty average one for the team, as we finished fourteenth. But it had been a personal success for me because I had been a constant fixture in West Ham's first team. I had not missed a single League or Cup game – and ended up top scorer with seventeen in the league, while Geoff Hurst and Pop Robson had eight each. Add in my cup goals and I ended up with 23 in all competitions, a more than satisfying return. Not bad for a kid who couldn't find the Boleyn Ground and got off at the wrong tube stop the day he arrived in drizzly England.

14

NEW PARTNERSHIPS

LOOKING BACK, I CONSIDER THIS PERIOD OF MY CAREER, THE early 1970s, as my prime; working with players like Geoff Hurst and Pop Robson, sensing moves, getting into scoring positions almost by instinct. I had also learned to use my height and weight to get my head on to many of Harry Redknapp's crosses. Harry was no bit-part player. He may be best known as a manager but he made around 170 appearances for West Ham and was a great crosser of the ball. He was like a little whippet as he raced to the by-line and then picked you out. I knew that if I could keep those partnerships then West Ham could only go from strength to strength. I'm glad in a way that I didn't know in the close season of 1972 that both Geoff and Harry were on their way out of West Ham – Geoff to Stoke, Harry to Bournemouth. It would have ruined my summer.

When I learned that these team-mates were to be sold, I wondered what was going on – and so did a lot of Hammers' fans. Strikers learn to read each other's moves: they have to. In professional football forwards get a fraction of a second to set up or score a goal. They have to be ready to receive a pass, a flick, a header, in less time than it takes to draw breath, especially in situations where one striker is standing with his back to goal.

I had perfected moves on the training ground with Geoff Hurst that we put into practice during games. Many of the moves came instinctively, however. That is what separates the good players from the great: that natural ability to carve out or take a chance, react instinctively. I'm not trying in any way to be arrogant here. I'd never write here or anywhere else that I was a 'great' player. That's for others to decide in terms of the company I played with. Let's just say I'd like to think that, coming from an island the size of Bermuda, and having to build a career thousands of miles from home, took some commitment in those days as well as perhaps a spot of courage. How many people would have embarked on something that they had no idea would work out or not?

I felt uneasy about the departures of Harry and Geoff. Both were good friends of mine and now they were considered surplus to requirements. Geoff had scored 248 goals in 499 games and I personally believe he left too early. He had done so much for the club. Maybe Ron was looking to the future and considered that I could fill straight in as our target man who would hold the ball up. But playing with your back to goal is hard. Having Geoff around helped all us guys up front. I was still young and learning the game, and I needed to learn more about forward play from Geoff as well as Pop. Also, while defenders had been worrying about Geoff and his reputation, they gave *me* more space.

Harry, meanwhile, left for Bournemouth, where he spent the next four years. He hadn't been able to nail down a regular place and wanted a fresh challenge. It's strange when you see people all the time and all of a sudden they're not there. That's the sad thing about the profession in the modern era. You can meet someone today and they'll be gone tomorrow. Despite two of my dearest teammates leaving, I had to stay focused and get myself in top physical condition again. I made full use of Bermuda's pink beaches, pounding along them in the early mornings before the full heat of the day built up – even so, I would be drenched with sweat by the time I'd run 100 yards.

It didn't take long for me to score my first goal of the 1972/73 campaign, the second game in fact, on a dreary Monday evening at home to Coventry City. The problem was that the entire Coventry defence violently disagreed with the ref's decision to award the goal and surrounded him in protest. I had got my head to a cross and nodded it firmly towards goal. Bill Glazier, the Coventry keeper, got a hand to it but somehow the ball span back over his shoulder before one of the defenders scrambled it clear – and that seemed to be that.

Suddenly we all noticed the linesman on the far side signalling that the ball had crossed the line. The referee ran across to him then pointed towards the centre circle, indicating that we had scored. There was pandemonium, with the Coventry players making their opinions known in no uncertain terms. I was surprised that none of them were sent off. You should always go along with what the officials say. The Coventry players should have gone back to the halfway line straight away and kicked off. Referees deserve a medal for some of the unruly conduct they have to put up with, whether in my day or today when the pressures are even greater. It all makes the need for goal-line technology all the more pressing at as many levels of the game as possible. Referees are only human, they make mistakes. Technology is the right way to go. I'm all in favour of extending it to other decisions like contentious penalties and offside. I know this is being actively considered by the game's lawmakers and I hope it comes into effect.

For keeping super-fit, understanding and applying the laws of the game, standing up to ninety minutes of strain and stress, being asked to make the correct call in a split second, putting up with verbal abuse from managers, players and supporters: for all of this, referees back then were paid the princely sum of £10.50 per match. And the linesmen? They received half that amount. At least the officials were spared instant replays, which highlight every single mistake and which nowadays are scrutinised by fans and television pundits alike.

I have to also applaud the cameramen – or make that a single cameraman – recording for those early editions of *Match of the Day*. They were simply amazing. They had to cover every piece of the action from goalmouth scrambles to long balls, all with limited resources developed years previously. They had no digital 'zooms' or portable touchline video equipment. Sometimes they operated under really difficult conditions, producing excellent footage even when a thick fog rolled in from the River Thames, almost obscuring the entire pitch.

After the Coventry game, I felt pretty confident about the rest of the season and that I could go on another goal-scoring run if I stayed clear of injury. It was not to be. The goals were being banged in, but not by me. By November that season West Ham were leading the way in goals scored in the First Division. The problem was, I hadn't got many of them.

Even the London tabloid newspapers were starting to take note. One columnist wrote that 'while West Ham have overcome the handicap of losing the powerful skills of one of football's front runners, Clyde Best has struggled.' The article went on: 'This season there is no Hurst, and not many goals for Best.

Perhaps Best has missed Hurst more than West Ham have as a team.'

I'm pretty sure we paid more attention to what the papers wrote about us in my day than they do now. After all, we knew a lot of the reporters by their first name. Sometimes we even socialised with them. I remember reading this particular article and thinking to myself: 'What would my goals tally be by now if Hursty had stayed?' The trouble was, if truth be told, I wasn't the same player once Geoff left. Playing as a target man didn't suit me. Still, there was nothing I could do about it. I was a professional footballer and simply had to get on with the job.

Some games stick out from that season, however. Once again it involved a long train ride, this time to Everton for a league game. This wasn't just 'any old league game' – it was Bobby Moore's 500th appearance for West Ham. Goodison Park was packed for the occasion and before kick-off Bobby was presented with a decanter by the Everton officials.

Everton were without Joe Royle, one of the best strikers in England, but they still came fast out of the traps. Disaster struck after only five minutes when Frank Lampard took a knock and had to go off after tackling Bernie Wright. Young Kevin Lock came on and Bobby nursed him superbly through the rest of the game.

I remember that Bernie Wright – a player notorious among Everton supporters as one of the worst in the club's history – was in good form for the Toffees. Twice he went close with good efforts. Both he and John Connolly were putting our defence under pressure and Bernie got his head to a Connolly cross and bulleted the ball past Bobby Ferguson.

We were not playing that badly, gradually working our way back into the game, and we were rewarded almost on the stroke of half-time. Dudley Tyler swung over a corner which Trevor Brooking finished off to silence the Everton crowd.

I had been getting some racist stick from a section of the crowd but I was determined it was not going to upset me. About fifteen minutes into the second half I took a pass from Bobby Moore just inside my own half. I looked up but couldn't see a team-mate free. Next second, an Everton player tackled me but I kept my balance and still had the ball at my feet. I kept moving. Another tackle. I brushed it off and headed towards the Everton goal. Next I felt my jersey being tugged by Terry Darracott. Surely the ref would blow for a foul, I thought – but he didn't!

I kept going. Peter Scott came roaring in on me from the right-back position but he was too late. David Lawson, the Everton goalie, came running out, trying to narrow the angle, but he was too late as well. I pulled the trigger and watched the net bulge. GOAL! I had scored the winner against one of England's top teams in Bobby Moore's anniversary game. What a feeling. Suddenly the racist chanting stopped and I could hear some of the Everton fans applauding me.

*

IN THOSE DAYS, AS A BLACK PLAYER, NO MATTER WHERE YOU went you would be in for a hard time. You just had to tough it out. Most teams gave me stick away from home as soon as I ran onto the field. Sorry to repeat myself, but I always tried to remember what my dad told me: I was playing for those who were to come after me. It was one of the best pieces of advice I ever had. I had to adapt to my surroundings, simple as that. But there is little doubt that temperament played a big part. I tell people all the time that if I had acted up and kept losing my cool, I think it would have more difficult for the black players who followed me in terms of image. Bring able to deal with situations was something I always seemed to have a penchant for. Good thing I did.

I know some say I was too gentle on the pitch. Just like Gary Lineker several years later, I was never sent off in my professional career. And I can't remember being booked more than three or four times. I'm quite proud of that record. What do I put it down to? Well, for a start, showing my temper was never in my nature. I could always stand up for myself but quite frankly I wasn't the Joe Jordan type. That just wasn't my style. No offence to Joe, he was a very good striker, but we all look after ourselves in different ways. Being a striker I wasn't really into tackling people, but there is no question my size helped me. I was big but I wasn't aggressive. If I got kicked I got up, dusted myself down and just carried on. If someone came in hard on me, chances are they would end up hurting themselves more than me! I never got in referees' faces or players' faces. Unlike people such as the lad at Chelsea now, Diego Costa. He's a terrific talent but, for goodness' sake, every five minutes he's in the referee's face. The game shouldn't be played that way. If you're a good player, let your boots do the talking. Back in the day, he'd never have got away with some of the things he does.

I know some of my old team-mates like Trevor Brooking believe I should have imposed myself more, that if I reacted more often I might have been more successful. But I knew what the rewards were for me and how I had to attain them. I liked to play with touch and running off the ball, rather than using my physique. Many people have said they think I was too shy, but those that go round shooting their mouths off are not usually the ones who live up to their billing. I never saw much point in talking when there wasn't much to say. And let's face it, I had come to England as a teenager from a far-off land to play on the same stage as some of the best players of my generation. I was always taught to be polite. I always thought that entertaining people was the right way. I couldn't let racism destroy my game. I had to win my own battles. And what would have happened if I had struck out? Maybe I would have been dismissed. How would that have helped the team? Being remembered as big, strong and gentle? That's OK by me.

If I had to pick out another game where the racist taunts came thick and fast it would be playing at Leicester one season. The supporters were right on my back, dishing out some terrible abuse. I responded in the best way I knew how: by scoring. A spin, a shot and watching as the ball sailed into the net to set us up with a 1–0 win. The racist slurs from the Leicester supporters suddenly drained away.

For West Ham fans, as well as my team-mates at the time, race or the colour of a person's skin was never an issue – and, as I've said a million times, the best way to silence those kinds of chants was to ram it down their throats by sticking the ball in the net.

During the European Championship finals in the Ukraine in 2012 I heard all kinds of racist chanting going on. I was only watching on television but you could hear it plain as daylight. Why don't FIFA and UEFA tell participating countries that their teams will be thrown out of competitions if their supporters abuse players? That would soon stop them. What kind of message are they sending to children and families who are watching the games on television? I bet closing down a few stadiums would soon put a halt to the abuse.

This is a big concern of mine. England may set an example these days to the rest of the world when it comes to racial tolerance, but in some parts of eastern Europe – and even in some western counties like Italy – they are at the stage where English football was thirty-odd years ago.

Players shouldn't have to go through that. There was a lot of coverage of that incident back in January 2013 when the whole Milan team, led by Kevin-Prince Boateng, walked off the pitch in protest at the racist chanting by the fans of the team they were playing in a mid-season friendly. The game had to be abandoned. I can't help thinking, good for them. I'd like to think that if it were me in that situation, playing today, I'd have done exactly the same thing. But it would never have happened in my day, though it would have been interesting to see the reaction. You have to make a stand somewhere. The truth is, some people find it easier to take the abuse than others.

Eastern European fans have to understand not to judge a person by the colour of his skin. And that includes Russia, where we have the World Cup in 2018. The way to hurt those clubs and countries with a racist element among their supporters is, as I say, to make them play behind closed doors. They might then be more willing to act, once their revenue is hit hard. The authorities simply have to take more responsibility, too. It's not enough just to have banners at matches saying, 'Keep Racism out of Football'. What is actually being done to make this happen?

I have one idea. Why not enlist the help of established black players to visit those countries with the biggest problem, to talk to the fans, let them see that the colour of someone's skin doesn't make them any different, that once you play this game, the ball doesn't care where you come from and neither should the fans. I would be prepared to consider such a role but I'm not holding my breath that I'll ever be asked. I believe there are a number of officials in FIFA who shy away from giving real jobs to real football people because they want to control everything. Look at my own region, for instance. What a mess politically. Bermuda is part of CONCACAF, which is the FIFA confederation that covers North and Central America and the Caribbean. We've had more corrupt people than you could shake a stick at. Proper sports people don't behave like that and I'd like to see more of them in positions of power. They would soon tell you if you were doing something wrong, rather than take the easy option of just going with the flow and keeping quiet.

I'm really not comfortable with the means by which some people in the game end up in positions of authority. The head of our national association in

Bermuda, Larry Mussenden, is a big wheel in FIFA, head of the appeals committee. Larry has also put his name forward for president of CONCACAF. But Larry is a lawyer rather than a sports administrator. Imagine what would happen if I went knocking on his office door and said, 'Come on, let me be a lawyer too.' I'd get laughed out of town. Understandably so, because I'm not qualified. So how come all these guys are suddenly qualified to run football if they haven't been involved in the game itself? I'd like to see more ex-footballers playing a bigger role running the sport and stop letting people from the outside come in and do it. We've been there, we know first-hand what is required.

I've always thought that those who have actually played sport are likely to command greater respect among the public and have a cleaner moral background than the businessmen fat cats who get lucky by being parachuted in to run the game but who have no experience – and no ethics. There have been a lot more soccer players who have never got into trouble than those who have. Sport in general turns out good people. But can you really say that good people are administering the game these days? Look at the Cayman Islands banker and (now disgraced) football official Jeffrey Webb. When he took over at CONCA-CAF, everyone thought he was ideal. He was even being touted as a potential FIFA president. Here we had a black administrator with a seemingly whiter than white past, telling everyone how he wanted to clean up FIFA. Next minute he is arrested as part of a huge FBI-led racketeering investigation! It was pure double standards, but I wasn't really shocked. Webb replaced the notorious Jack Warner – perhaps the biggest crook of them all – promising all kinds of changes. A new dawn. Yet many of his people were the same old faces. The fact that Webb at first pleaded not guilty, then guilty when he was caught up in the FIFA corruption scandal and had to put up $10 million for his bail including cars and watches, tells you everything you need to know about the severity of his crimes.

In life there are two ways – a right way and a wrong way. When you start moving between the two, that's when you have problems. When you look at the way the wealth spread is distributed around CONCACAF, it's pretty disgraceful. So many footballers in the Caribbean simply don't know where their next meal is coming from. That's the truth. Yet we allow the bigwigs to help themselves to more and more at the players' expense. So many of FIFA and CONCACAF guys have walked around for too long with big cigars and drinking champagne while the players get nothing. Why don't we in Bermuda have the same facilities as in, say, Trinidad? Maybe it's got something to do with Warner who is from Trinidad and is notorious as one of the most self-serving and corrupt football officials in the game's history.

I'm not a FIFA expert but I read the papers, listen to the radio, monitor the Internet and watch the television. I applaud the reform process FIFA has promised. But please, let's even out the money more reasonably so that everyone gets a fair share. If you build a sports complex in Trinidad, make sure other areas of CONCACAF are treated the same way. The confederation's role is supposed to make sure all the countries in the region are developed properly and, as far as I can see, that hasn't happened. Every place in the region should have decent pitches, not just one or two countries. To understand why that is not the case, you need to understand the geopolitics of the area and the fact that too much power was in the hands of too few people. And that takes us directly back to Warner. He should have made sure, in all those years in charge, that the whole of Central America and the Caribbean were given the facilities they needed with the funds available, but the extent to which the man who for so long was FIFA's most prominent CONCACAF official lined his own pockets beggars belief. Warner is no friend of Bermuda, believe me. He needs to take a lot of responsibility for how poor some of our facilities are. It's a sad indictment of all his years in charge of our region that he ended up being one of those accused of bribery by the US justice authorities. Clearly he was serving his own interests rather than caring a jot about trying to develop football in the parts of his confederation that needed it the most. He seems to have taken a lot of people for a ride. I wouldn't trust Warner or any of his cronies as far as I can throw them. Most people in football, at least those I have come across, have an opinion of Warner and it isn't very good. We just can't continue with people taking advantage because, in the end, hard-working fans won't come to matches if they feel those running the sport are corrupt. The players and fans should always come first – and that means giving them the best possible facilities. During the February 2016 FIFA presidential election we heard all kinds of stuff about giving football back to the people, about restoring trust. Sometimes those in high places tend to forget how important this is. What has been going on at FIFA is, quite frankly, scandalous.

*

THROUGHOUT THE 1972/73 SEASON I'D BEEN MAKING ARRANGE-
ments to move out of my home-from-home and bid farewell to the Charles
family. They had made me feel so welcome for so many years. I had run up an
astronomical phone bill to Bermuda every week calling Alfreida, my girlfriend
back home, and we decided there was no point being separated any longer.

I wouldn't say it had been love at first sight between us, but suffice to say I
could see the attraction at an early age. Very early. Just eight, in fact! We came
from the same parish and we first met at primary school. Years went by before we
bumped into each other again. I had come home one summer for a wedding and
there she was. I'm not sure she remembered me but I certainly remembered her.
I was about nineteen and we immediately started dating. I'd had a lot of female
friends but no girlfriend as such. She was the one who immediately caught my
eye and pretty soon came over to England to visit me. At the end of the 1972/73
season, around eight months after meeting again, both of our mums travelled
from Bermuda to London and we were married at Lewisham Registry Office on
10 May. My brother Carlton was my best man, while Alfreida had Norma Mills
as her maid of honour. I had some Greek friends who owned a steakhouse in
Leicester Square and we had the reception there. It was a pretty low-key affair
because it was the end of the season and things were winding down. There was
no time for any honeymoon because we had to get our new home ready.

I had already been house-hunting in the London area and found a beautiful
flat in Woodhaven Gardens, Ilford, not too far from Chadwell Heath. While it
was bliss to move in with my new wife, it was naturally a wrench to leave the
Charles abode. Clive and John have both passed on now but I always try to call
their sister Rita as often as I can. As I've said elsewhere in the book, Clive and
I were like brothers in those first years in London, we did everything together.
We went to clubs, we went to pubs, we'd go to movies, out for dinner, out for
lunch. In future years we got back together when I went to play in Portland in
the United States, of which more later. When Clive died of prostate cancer in
2003, after a two-year battle against the disease, at the tragically young age of
51 – ironically, the same age as Bobby Moore – I was devastated, all the more so
as it was just a year and six days after his brother John also passed away, likewise

struck down by cancer. I went over to see Clive while he was ill but wasn't able to get back again for the funeral, which hit me hard. We'd had another of those terrible storms and there were no flights out of the island. But I'm sure he's up there looking down on me. 'If you're there, man, I couldn't possibly have got to where I am without you.'

By the time the new season started, I was given all kinds of stick about being overweight. Some might put it down to Alfreida's cooking, but it wasn't so much her as my sister-in-law, who had come over for the summer. Romaine made these amazing pies. Outside in the garden we had peach, plum and apple trees and she kept making these pies while I was watching the cricket on television. I just couldn't help myself. I'll never forget going back to training and Ernie Gregory, one of the West Ham coaches, exclaiming, 'Besty, what on earth have you been doing?' Ernie took no prisoners and when I explained about the fruit pies, I was put in a plastic sweat suit and had to run through Epping Forest keeping up with Ernie on his bicycle. It was hell, but I had to shed the extra weight, which took me around two or three weeks. I learned from that never to indulge myself in pre-season again.

15

BRILLIANT COMEBACK TO RESERVES

BY THE 1973/74 SEASON I WASN'T SCORING GOALS ON A REGU-
lar basis. I was still only 22, but it seemed at times as if I had 'peaked too early'
in my career: I will never know. It was not a question of being overweight or out
of shape or having the wrong kind of diet or anything like that. To his credit,
Ron Greenwood kept playing me in every game, and to improve my balance and
timing, I even went to *dancing lessons*.

Pop Robson's father-in-law, Len Heppell, was a dancing and balance special-
ist and once a week he would come to our training ground where he would put
me through a series of exercises designed to improve my weight distribution,
pivoting and balance. He said I was quick but could be quicker. Pop was always
down on his backside and up in a flash. I wanted to be more like that, despite
my build. The lessons worked. I felt a lot more confident, especially in the rough
and tumble of the penalty area and six-yard box.

My form had been up and down but the boss included me in the team
selected to play Chelsea at Stamford Bridge, another of those Christmas derbies
that I loved. Chelsea have always been a formidable club even in the days when
they weren't winning trophies as they are now. They have always had a special
feel about them for visiting teams. They may have had a lean period before
Roman Abramovich bought the club, but in the 1970s they were the most
fashionable side in the country, reflecting the cultural trends of the era, with the
iconic King's Road a stone's throw from their stadium.

On Boxing Day 1973 we boarded the team coach at Upton Park en route to the 'posh' part of the city, past Oxford Street and Regent Street, all lit up for Christmas, and Trafalgar Square with its traditional massive Christmas tree. The journey on our team bus from Upton Park to Stamford Bridge used to fascinate me. I loved the East End. There was a warm cheeriness about that part of London. People in the shipyards and factories still lined up outside pay offices and received cash in hand on Friday nights.

As the bus wound its way towards Stamford Bridge, I couldn't help but marvel at some of the houses in and around Kensington. Some of the dwellings had little railings outside with gold-painted tops – like small spears. There were brass polished signs on many of the doors and even the pubs looked really posh, with tables and chairs outside, almost like private restaurants.

As our coach neared the ground we could see our supporters pouring out of the underground or trying to cram into the nearby pubs for a final pint before kick-off. Over the past few years I have watched so many foreign mercenaries saturate the English game with massive salaries and fat contracts. Well, on that chilly Boxing Day at Stamford Bridge in front of a full house we had 22 of some of the best British players on display – or perhaps I should say 21 plus one Bermudian!

Chelsea had in their team a stack of experienced England players including Peter Bonetti, Ron Harris, Alan Hudson and Peter Osgood. I'm not sure if all Chelsea supporters actually knew Ron's first name, given his nickname of Chopper. He was a fearsome defender, despite his relatively small stature, 100 per cent committed to his team. He was hard as nails but, contrary to popular belief, he was never a dirty player. He once came on holiday to Bermuda and, like so many footballers of our generation, he was the opposite to how he came across as a player. I played against Ron so many times and forged a solid friendship with him.

When we ran down the tunnel onto the pitch the noise level increased so much that we could hardly hear ourselves shout to each other. I was grateful to the gaffer for having included me in the team. Bobby Gould had arrived from Bristol City a couple of months earlier for £80,000 and was playing alongside me.

Chelsea had us straight on the back foot and our supporters were stunned into silence when first Ian Britton then Alan 'Huddy' Hudson put them 2–0 ahead at the interval. When we got back to the changing room at half-time Ron tore into us. He wasn't the explosive type but on this occasion he was extremely displeased and told us we were as good a team as Chelsea and there was no way we should be two goals behind. That settled it. With the Chelsea supporters in full voice we came out for the second half with our sleeves rolled up.

Five minutes into the second half Frank Lampard crashed home a pass from Trevor Brooking. The turning point came just after Osgood hit the underside of the bar for Chelsea. Right after that we went up to their end and equalised through Bobby Gould. It was 2–2! Three minutes later I put us in front when Trevor Brooking crossed and I got my head on it, and six minutes from time I scored with another header, this time from a Bobby Gould cross. We had scored three times in eleven minutes and were unstoppable. As comebacks go, it was one of the greatest of my career.

We were a cheery lot, some fortified by beer, as we boarded the bus back to the East End – at least most of us were. I remembering swivelling round in my seat and looking out the back window as we pulled out of the parking lot. Most of the floodlights were out in the stadium, leaving only enough illumination for the ground staff to repair divot marks on the pitch. As Stamford Bridge disappeared from view, I began to wonder if I would ever play there again.

By now, I was no longer a regular in the first team. Ted McDougall had been signed from Manchester United but had contributed very little and left soon after following a dust-up with Billy Bonds. We were playing at Leeds and Billy, being the no-nonsense guy he was, made his feelings known in no uncertain terms to Ted when we came off after losing. Billy couldn't bear other players not pulling their weight – as far as he saw it. He expected everyone else to give their all too and he didn't think Ted was doing that. He gripped hold of Ted and a few of us had to physically restrain Billy from doing any damage. He was a serious type of person and wanted everyone to put in the same effort as him. He was a fantastic professional but couldn't bear the thought of anyone slacking off.

Personally I got on well with Ted and so did the likes of Frank Lampard and Graham Paddon. But Ted wasn't one for being involved in the patient build-up football we liked to play. He just wasn't the type. He wanted to throw himself at direct balls into the box. Even without Ted, Bobby Gould was competing with Pop Robson and myself for one of the striking spots and the bottom line was that I was no longer guaranteed first-team football.

*

PLAYING IN THE RESERVES CAN BE A DEPRESSING EXPERIENCE. IT is an excellent avenue for younger players to develop their skills playing alongside seasoned professionals who are recovering from injury and playing their way back to fitness. As an eighteen-year-old learning my profession I used to love being involved in those games, listening to the old hands as they shouted to each other. Then it was a whole new experience as a raw teenager from Bermuda, an understandable stepping stone. I would come off the pitch exhausted – but exhilarated as well. My all-round game improved rapidly in that first year. Reserve games were the catalyst I needed to hone and improve the skills I needed.

But going the 'other way', so to speak – back into the reserves from the first team – is no one's idea of fun. Most players have to go through it at some point in their careers – unless you are Lionel Messi or Cristiano Ronaldo. I hated going back into the reserves but I was not going to let it get me down and was determined not to stay there long. Travelling across London to a deserted Highbury on a rainy winter's afternoon is not exactly an uplifting experience. There is only emptiness all around: empty parking lot, empty terraces, empty stands. Often there would be parents, relatives and friends come to these games to check on the progress of the younger players, but overall we were always conscious that the first team was what it was all about, whether at Anfield, White Hart Lane or Elland Road. At half-time and full time in reserve games we all waited anxiously to hear the scores from the main games up and down the country. And if the West Ham first team hadn't done well we would all sit and think to ourselves: if only my name had been on the team sheet, that result would never have happened.

One bonus we did always have after away reserve games was when the coach stopped at the nearest fish and chip shop. There's nothing like a fish supper on a winter's evening in England – with extra salt and vinegar, of course. Everyone loved it.

Luckily, I was only in the reserves for a couple of weeks. John Lyall saw I was training well and let the gaffer know. Sometimes players simply don't understand the pressure on coaches. If a player's head isn't in it, it doesn't make sense to keep picking him because he will let you down. My head was always in it. I just needed to get my confidence back. Football, as they always say, is a results-driven business. The buck always stops with the manager – just look at the number of sackings there are. The point I'm trying to make is that players have always let managers down. Some of them don't care two hoots about whether the coach is going to be there at the end of the season or not.

*

PLAYING POORLY, HOWEVER, IS VERY DIFFERENT FROM BEING RELegated, yet that's exactly what happened to Manchester United at the end of the 1973/74 season. When we played them that January they seemed to be more interested in a physical battle than playing football. It was not as if they lacked quality players, not with internationals such as Jim Holton and Sammy McIlroy in their ranks. It was just that they wanted to get the boot in more than play the ball. I was disappointed by that.

When the game started it was obvious that it was going to be hard and physical. I was very lucky with injuries throughout my career but in this game I could have been severely crocked. I remember taking a pass from Billy Bonds and turning towards goal when 'WHAM!' – Martin Buchan, the Scottish international defender, came sliding in for a challenge. I'm surprised I didn't break both legs and land on top of a number 5 bus passing along Green Street at the time. The fact I was not badly hurt – or hurt at all – was a miracle. The newspaper snappers got a picture of the tackle in question and one report described Buchan, probably United's most influential player for a decade, as 'Machine Gun Martin'. It was that kind of game and I'm afraid to say they got to us so badly that we got stuck right into them as well. It was a real battle, hardly the best advertisement for the beautiful game. The only one of their team who seemed to want to play football that day was George Graham, who of course made his name with Arsenal both as a player and manager. The rest didn't seem to care and just kept sticking the boot in. Billy Bonds put us ahead, Sammy McIlroy equalised and Pat Holland gave us the points when he nodded home the winner. It was the most unsporting Manchester United team I had ever played against.

You may have noticed that I cared a lot about sportsmanship. People ask me where I got that attitude from. We all like to win, but you have to learn to lose gracefully too. I was always like that, even at school. I was never disrespectful to my sport.

When we opened the newspapers next morning there were two pictures of the game alongside the report – and I was in both, being 'clattered' by various defenders. One report, referring to the Manchester United tactics, simply said 'Good riddance: the First Division is better off without Manchester United.' In the end they finished second bottom, though we were not that far above them, finishing eighteenth.

Some fixtures always seem to be more memorable than others. Perhaps it's just the 'chemistry' – or lack of it – between certain teams. West Ham seemed to have had that with Everton whenever I played against them. When they came down to play us in February 1974 their line-up had changed dramatically. Gone were Peter Scott, Henry Newton, John Connolly, Rod Belfitt and Bernie Wright. More significantly, Howard Kendall had gone to Birmingham City.

The team sheet they handed to the ref that day included the debut appearance of Britain's costliest player at the time: Bob Latchford. The price tag was a mere £350,000. I wonder what his value would be now. Bob was one excellent striker – good with his head, both feet, physically strong, with excellent timing. There was a lot of pre-match publicity about Bob and his expensive tag but we were playing well at the time and were not conceding many goals.

Within five minutes of kick-off, we knew we were in a game – and all because of Bob. He headed on Micky Buckley's pass to winger George Telfer, who nodded it home. We were stunned – and worse was to follow. Terry Darracott, with whom I'd had plenty of skirmishes, took a free kick which our goalie Mervyn Day could not quite reach and Telfer hit it in from close range. Upton Park went very quiet.

We found ourselves two down within twenty minutes. That's when Billy Bonds took the game by the scruff of the neck. His work rate was amazing, his passing a joy to watch. And we profited accordingly. Graham Paddon, a recent West Ham signing from Norwich, pulled one back on 33 minutes, then Trevor Brooking and Keith Coleman combined well to set me up and I cracked home the equaliser.

We were all square at half-time and we tore into Everton in the second half. I battered home a cross not long after the restart, but they immediately equalised:

3–3. We summoned up our last reserves of strength on a mudbath of a pitch and it was fitting that Billy Bonds should bag the winning goal five minutes from time, powering home a corner. The whole stadium went wild. Those kinds of games gave me many precious memories of my West Ham years. As a bonus, I was voted Man of the Match that day.

ALTHOUGH WE FINISHED THE SEASON EIGHTEENTH, THERE WAS no doubting our attack-minded approach. There were only five other teams that scored more than our 55 goals that season. That shows we were exciting to watch. The problem was obviously in defence: we conceded approximately twice as many goals as either Liverpool or Leeds. But then so did Ipswich – and they finished fourth!

16

MISSING OUT ON FA CUP GLORY

ON 5 SEPTEMBER 1974 OUR BEAUTIFUL DAUGHTER KIMBERLEY WAS born at Ilford Maternity Hospital in Redbridge. She weighed seven pounds and Alfreida and I were overjoyed at the arrival of our precious little bundle. Footballers always say having a child changes their life and I can't disagree. It gave me added responsibility and having a daughter made it all the more special. Well, you know how daughters cling to their dads! I must say, I have found that out over the years – even now that Kimberley has grown up and has a successful career in insurance having studied at universities in both the UK (law) and America (English). I'm so proud of her. We are very close.

I was in and out of the first team once again and still training hard, always doing my best. But there was one massive void. Ron Greenwood, the man who nurtured me, helped me cope with all those racist chants, picked me up when I was down and all but made me the player I became, was no longer manager. Under growing pressure from fans frustrated at our lack of success, Ron had 'moved upstairs', as they say, and John Lyall had now stepped into his shoes to become the main gaffer. Managers come and go, of course they do, but Ron had thirteen years at Upton Park and was part of the fabric of the club, rather like Alex Ferguson was at Manchester United and Arsene Wenger at Arsenal.

Players, however, simply have to adapt to whoever is in charge and, to be fair, it wasn't as if West Ham brought in some stranger from outside with no previous affinity with the club and its way of playing. John Lyall was not dissimilar to

Ron in terms of personality and had risen through the ranks to take over, a position he ended up holding for the best part of fifteen years. One difference was that he could give you a right rollicking if he didn't think you were doing the business. But I can't really say a bad word about John. After all, he was in charge of the youth team when I first went to England and he took a gamble on me. Players sometimes tend to make excuses about coaches not playing them. But if you're not playing well, you are not going to be picked. I will always have a special place in my heart for John.

One of his first moves after replacing Ron was to pay Rochdale £40,000 for Alan Taylor, who signed for us on his 21st birthday. And what an impact he made in his first season. In only his fifth game, he scored both goals for us in the sixth round of the FA Cup at Highbury when we defeated Arsenal in front of a crowd of 56,000 fans to reach the semi-final, then he got another brace as we defeated Ipswich town 2–1 at Stamford Bridge in the semi-final replay.

The rest is history: an all-London cup final against Fulham, even though they were a division below. I knew pretty much straight away that I would not be playing. I had only played in one round of the cup run, against third-tier Swindon, scoring in neither the first game which we drew 1–1 nor the replay when we edged home 2–1. A section of the fans had clearly turned against me and I was continually barracked in the first game at Upton Park. Afterwards, Jim Barron, the tall Swindon keeper, made a point of publicly telling the fans to lay off me, which was nice. You just have to soldier on.

Alan Taylor's arrival had pushed me even further down the pecking order and, while I'd be lying if I said I wasn't gutted about not being picked for Wembley, as I say, it was no surprise when I wasn't on the team sheet. To have picked up a cup winner's medal would have been the absolute highlight of my career and I guess it's probably my only regret. Today the whole squad gets a medal regardless of whether you play or not. I wasn't even substitute – Bobby Gould sneaked in ahead of me – but at least I got to walk on the pitch in my cup final suit. I shouldn't really complain because most players never even get near the place. At the end of the day, the Lord doesn't care how many medals you had. You can't take them with you, after all.

One of the weirdest things about the final was seeing Bobby Moore in a black and white Fulham strip instead of West Ham claret and blue. Bobby had played his last game for us in the previous season's FA Cup at Hereford (who we'd been drawn against for the second year in a row), where he got injured. That was in January 1974, and two months later he was allowed to leave after more than fifteen years' loyal service, taking with him the club record for appearances, since overtaken by Billy Bonds. I personally felt Bobby left too early, the same as Geoff Hurst. The pair of them meant so much to the club – and to me. When you're young you look up to people like that and I have never looked up to any players more than Bobby and Hursty. I have since read that Bobby left West Ham on bad terms and was never again fully welcomed at the club. If that's the case, it's disgraceful, though I didn't know it at the time. To me, the way he carried himself throughout my time at West Ham was an inspiration. Whatever happened between Bobby and the management in his latter days, it's a shame that personalities can get sometimes in the way. I wish Bobby had been able to work things out. His name is still mentioned today like he never left at all.

A few years ago I attended a reception and dinner in England to celebrate black players. I was introduced as 'the legend'. People like Cyrille Regis and Luther Blissett came up to me and said that I had been their inspiration when they were kids. It made me feel proud. As I said before, I was never sent off once in my professional career. I never retaliated or put myself in a position where the ref would have to send me off or, after they were introduced to the English game in 1976, pull out a red card. I kept my cool and got on with the game. Where did I learn that from? Bobby Moore. Bobby got stick from rival fans all the time. Why? Because he never got upset, never lost his cool, never became heated. It was because he was unflappable and never took the bait. It was nothing whatsoever, in my opinion at least, to do with that infamous incident in Bogota when Bobby was detained for four days after being accused of stealing a bracelet from a jewellery store located in the hotel in which the England team were staying in the build-up to the 1970 World Cup finals. Whatever other people may think about the incident, I know he never took that bracelet. Besides, he could afford to buy it ten times over. Bobby was always in control of himself and he taught me all about self-discipline and staying focused. I will always be grateful to him for that. He was a footballing genius, not just for the way he played, but the way in which he conducted himself too. I read that people in England have been pushing for him to receive a posthumous knighthood. Good idea. Long overdue.

He should have been Sir Bobby Moore long ago for what he contributed. Plus, he was a hell of a human being, one of the nicest people the Lord has put on this earth.

Bobby had been a Hammer since he was fifteen yet here he was on the opposition side. There was little to indicate that the teams played in different divisions as play flowed from one end of the pitch to the other. I sat in the stand willing on my Hammers colleagues and, as the cliché goes, kicking every ball, making every tackle and getting my head on every cross that came into the box. It exhausted me just to sit and watch.

On the pitch, Alan Taylor was once again our cup hero. Just after the hour mark he converted a Billy Bonds cross and five minutes later scored his second of the game to win us the trophy. Alan hardly played a game except cup ties but achieved legendary status for his unique contribution.

Half of Wembley went wild and gave us a rapturous ovation while the other half slowly slunk out of the stadium. I was so proud of the lads as Billy was presented with the famous old silver trophy. What a day for the East End of London. The stadium was a sea of claret and blue. Afterwards all the staff, players and officials went into London to celebrate, but halfway through the party I had to leave and get back to Ilford as quickly as I could.

All players have disappointments in their careers. The key is to pick yourself up and I had a new challenge on the horizon. Alfreida had started packing my bags in preparation for a long and career-defining journey. We had already made plans. Very early next morning I was at Heathrow waiting to board a flight for the USA.

17

WHERE EXACTLY IS TAMPA?

BOBBY GOULD'S INCLUSION AS SUB (WE ONLY HAD ONE IN those days) in the cup final had made me think more about the future. I was 24 now and it was tough not being part of the action at Wembley that day. Not that I didn't get on well with Bobby, because I did. In fact, the last time I was in England I was doing a radio show and he phoned in to have a chat. I can't hold it against Bob that he got in as sub instead of me.

I had thought about asking for a transfer. Wolverhampton Wanderers had an offer to buy me accepted. But I didn't want to go. I just couldn't see myself pulling on the jersey of another English club and having to perhaps line up against the team I had joined as a raw teenager. I guess I'm a little sentimental that way. Back in the day most players had a true affection for their club. I'm not sure that's the case any longer. It was good for the fans too because they could identify with the team.

Although I now had Kimberley to occupy my time, I still wanted to work, as there was nothing better than putting on a pair of boots. Jack Turner, who used to do a lot of scouting for Bill Nicholson, was my agent and he had an office in Plaistow not far from where I was living; he also represented several other players at the club. He had been contacted a couple of months before the cup final by Eddie Firmani, who had an eighteen-year playing career in Italy and England before moving into management, first at Charlton and then at the Tampa Bay Rowdies. Eddie had inquired whether I would be interested in moving to the

NASL – the North American Soccer League. Soccer? I blinked. In Bermuda we play *FOOTBALL*. In England I played *FOOTBALL*. In Europe everyone plays *FOOTBALL*.

But SOCCER? Then Jack mentioned Tampa Bay and I blinked again. I knew all about the leagues in England, Scotland, Holland, Italy etc. – but what on earth was this? I didn't even know they played the round-ball game seriously across the pond. After all, America was synonymous with baseball, American football and basketball.

But things were slowly changing. In 1967 the FIFA-sanctioned United Soccer Association, which consisted of entire European and South American teams brought over to the US and given local names, had been created along with the unsanctioned National Professional Soccer League. It has been suggested that the timing of the creation of both leagues was related to the amount of attention given throughout the English-speaking world to England's World Cup win the year before. But NPSL television ratings were appalling, with empty stadiums as well as undistinguished foreign players who were unfamiliar to American sports fans. As a result, the two leagues merged on 13 December 1967 to form the North American Soccer League (NASL).

To say there were teething problems is an understatement. In America, sport is big business and even when the two leagues became one there was a problem fitting commercial breaks into televised play – however ludicrous that may sound. Traditional American sports all have natural breaks. Not so soccer.

The executives of the television companies decided to create breaks but it was ridiculously contrived. During one of the early games in the NASL it was discovered that over half of the free kicks had been called so that the television company involved could fit in commercials.

But from small beginnings, the NASL gradually grew in popularity, and when Pelé came out of retirement in 1975 to play for the New York Cosmos, crowds of 70,000 were a familiar sight at the Meadowlands Stadium. Other world-famous names who came to the USA for the twilight of their careers included Franz Beckenbauer, who signed for Cosmos in 1977, and, two years earlier still, the 'other' Best – George – who arrived the same time as I did and went to the Los Angeles Aztecs. Also in 1975 the great Eusebio arrived to play for the Boston Minutemen before transferring to the Toronto Metros-Croatia.

Alfreida and I talked and talked about the Tampa offer, which – initially at least – was only a loan deal for the summer. The league commenced in April and ran for four months. I knew I'd be missing a couple of games but West Ham were prepared to let me go on loan while retaining my contract. We decided to go ahead. Tampa would take over my wages for the time I spent in the USA.

I remember the day when I cleaned out my locker at the boot room at Upton Park containing my belongings. Even though I was only going to the USA on loan – although as it turned out I ended up staying – I wondered what the future would hold for me. I still wasn't sure where Tampa was and I'm sure a lot of folks questioned whether I was making the right decision.

Tampa is actually a beautiful city on the western side of Florida facing the Gulf of Mexico. I travelled with the young Crystal Palace midfielder Mark Lindsay, who was also joining. When we arrived, we were met at the airport by representatives of the Rowdies, who treated us like royalty. The day-time highs in southern Florida in May are about 85°F and in June and July temperatures can reach 90°F, probably around 10 degrees hotter than the equivalent temperature in Bermuda. The day we left London I think the temperature was about 54°F. New culture, new country, new climate.

Eddie Firmani had certainly been around the block a few times. South African-born of Italian extraction, he had been the subject of a record transfer involving a British club when he joined Sampdoria and he later played for Inter Milan and Genoa. He was a very capable coach and I looked forward to working with him.

Yet I still wasn't sure of the standard of the game in America. One thing I did know: Tampa was certainly not the East End of London. I couldn't see any red London buses, pubs or rows of terraced housing. And, of course, the Americans drive on the 'wrong' side of the road. Instead of the small, narrow streets around Upton Park, I was confronted with a 'cross-town expressway' as massive as the M1.

Tampa was also an intersection for Interstate 75 and Interstate 4. These huge Interstate Highways criss-cross America. Odd-numbered ones run north–south while even-numbered ones run east–west.

America is huge, almost 3,000 miles from coast to coast, making it impossible to have one league covering the entire country. As a result the NASL was divided into four regional divisions, with teams such as Toronto and Boston in the North Division. Tampa was in the Eastern Division along with the likes of Baltimore, Philadelphia, Washington and Miami. The Central Division contained teams from places such as Denver, San Antonio and Dallas, cities which themselves were often 1,000 miles from each other. The Western Division was made up of teams primarily from the west coast including the Portland Timbers and San Jose Earthquakes.

The complete structure was:

North Division
Boston Minutemen, Toronto Metros-Croatia, New York Cosmos, Rochester Lancers, Hartford Bicentennials

Eastern Division
Tampa Bay Rowdies, Miami Toros, Washington Diplomats, Philadelphia Atoms, Baltimore Comets

Central Division
St Louis Stars, Chicago Sting, Denver Dynamos, Dallas Tornado, San Antonio Thunder

Western Division
Portland Timbers, Seattle Sounders, Los Angeles Aztecs, Vancouver Whitecaps, San Jose Earthquakes

Every time we played away from home we travelled by air. It was the only realistic way. Travel time between Tampa and San Jose, for instance, was approximately five and a half hours. And there I was still thinking that our three-hour train ride between Euston and Manchester to play the Red Devils took its toll.

The structure of the NASL was a bit like the set-up of the present day UEFA Champions League, with the eight top point-scoring teams from across the divisions competing in the playoffs. Our team training each day had to be over by mid-morning, otherwise we would have suffered from heatstroke. Eddie moulded us together into a powerful and efficient football (or should I say *soccer*) unit and we easily topped our section before disposing of Toronto and the Miami Toros on our way to the Soccer Bowl final.

Having been an ex-player himself and with three Italy caps to his credit,

Eddie knew the game extremely well and made a point of only bringing in players he thought he could trust. He allowed us to go out and express ourselves and at the time we had probably the best side in the league: people like Derek Smethurst, Johnny Boyle, Johnny Sissons and Stewart Scullion. It's a lot easier playing with players who understand what the boss wants done.

I wouldn't say winning the Eastern Division and getting to the Soccer Bowl final made up for being left out of the FA Cup final a few months earlier. Nothing can replace the disappointment of missing out playing on Wembley's hallowed turf – although the cup sadly doesn't seem to mean as much these days as it did when I was around. With there being so much money involved, everyone in England looks at the top four in the Premier League for success. I don't approve of coaches resting their best players for the FA Cup. If you are playing and playing well, you should want to carry that on in cup ties. Maybe I'm just from a different era, but perhaps the authorities could introduce some kind of fresh incentive, maybe give the FA Cup winners a Champions League place. Then you might bring some of the glamour and glitter back to how it used to be. Also, back in my day, to play at Wembley you had to be in a cup final. Nowadays there are all kinds of games there – semi-finals, playoffs etc. It's not so special as it used to be. But times change and I suppose you have to go along with it.

ALTHOUGH IT COULDN'T COMPARE WITH WEMBLEY, I WAS STILL really looking forward to the biggest game of the US season as we took on the Portland Timbers. The Soccer Bowl took place on 24 August 1975 at Spartan Stadium in San Jose, California. It was in fact the first NASL championship game to be known as that and was televised coast to coast.

Our supporters, bizarrely, were called 'fannies' – a play on the word fan, so I was told – and were made up mostly of college kids who came to watch us and generated a lively atmosphere with their songs and chants. One section called themselves the Village Idiots, while another group were labelled the Yellow Card Section! I have no idea why but they certainly generated lots of noise.

One television commentator whimsically referred to Portland as 'The Timber Wolves' because a couple of Wolverhampton Wanderers players were in the team, Peter Withe and Barry Powell. Their side also featured Ray Martin (Birmingham City), Willie Anderson (Cardiff), Tony Betts (Aston Villa) and Brian Godfrey (Newport), while we had our fair share of ex-pats too, including those I've mentioned like Mark Lindsay of Crystal Palace, John Sissons who had been at Chelsea, Johnny Boyle and Stewart Scullion, but also the likes of Paul Hammond and Stewart Jump. Obviously money played a part in why some players made the move but I can honestly say that in my case it was the excitement of going to a new country and experiencing a new way of life.

The game was actually a terrific end-to-end encounter. Peter Withe was fancied by the critics as the striker who would tear us apart. Even before he made a name for himself in England, Peter was banging in the goals across the pond. The big-bearded Liverpudlian had scored 17 goals and added 7 assists in 22 games to lead the Timbers to first place in their division and a tie (with Tampa) for the best record in the league at 16–6. His knack for scoring goals that summer made him a huge favourite with the Portland supporters, who nicknamed him 'The Mad Header' and 'The Wizard of Nod'.

But he couldn't do it when it mattered most and was marked out of the game by Stewart Jump while I, along with Arsene Auguste, got my name on the scoresheet in a famous 2–0 win.

People say there were no rivalries in the early days of professional football in the USA but that's so wrong. Tampa Bay playing Cosmos was like Manchester United versus Liverpool. I remember one game in particular in 1976. Pelé and Franz Beckenbauer had just joined Cosmos, who paid a lot of money for all their big stars, rather like Manchester City and Chelsea do now. We had thrashed them 5–1 in Tampa with the game shown live on television.

A few weeks later we had to go to New York for the return and I'll never forget it. We were 3–1 up and cruising, courtesy of a hat-trick by one Clyde Best. There was only one winner, or so it seemed. But when Cosmos came out for the second half, Pelé was like a man possessed. They ended up beating us 5–4 and he was just unstoppable. Mark Lindsay was supposed to be picking him up but in one particular move, Pelé ran from one penalty box to the other before passing out to the wing. As the ball came back in and before he even got his head to it Pelé shouted, 'GOAL!' I've never seen or heard that before or since, from anyone. It was extraordinary. How can you scream 'GOAL' before you actually score? Remarkable!

Some places we played were packed out but not all. There were cities that simply weren't really ready for professional soccer and the locals just weren't into it. You can't be paying millions of dollars for star names when the public simply aren't interested. That's why the league didn't survive. Now the game is really on the up with the advent of Major League Soccer. Everyone seems to want to get in on the act of building a 'franchise'. Even David Beckham.

After the demise of the NASL, the Americans did their homework properly. This this time they are building the house first rather than the roof. Bottom up instead of top down. Their youth system is probably as strong as anywhere in the world, and there are millions of kids playing now.

In all, I played fifteen games while on loan for the Rowdies and scored eight goals in a twelve-week period. Not bad going. I loved it there. America seemed to suit us. There was no racism for a start – not in soccer grounds, anyway, or anywhere around the sport. That's because the Americans were used to seeing black players in other sports like baseball and gridiron football. It was virtually the norm. We had a lovely rent-free apartment, a car provided by the club and three swimming pools in the complex. Everything you could wish for. But by August it was all over. I closed the door of the apartment behind me, took a last look at the place, handed in my car keys and made my way to the airport.

18

FINAL FAREWELL

SUDDENLY, PERHAPS FOR THE FIRST TIME, I WAS UNSURE HOW MY career would pan out. I was no longer a seventeen-year-old from Somerset, Bermuda, travelling to London with stars in my eyes. I was 24, married and had a little girl. I had to plan for the future because I knew I had a fight on my hands to get back in the first team at West Ham.

When we landed at Heathrow it was grey and miserable. London children were returning to school once more after the summer holidays. Suddenly the streets seemed horribly narrow and tiny. I guess I kind of realised there and then that before too long I'd be returning to the States, where everything seemed fresh and exciting.

Meantime, Alfreida, Kimberley and myself settled back into life in Ilford. I thought I was in good physical condition. Playing over the summer in the sweltering heat of Florida had got me even fitter. As I buckled down to training, there was talk of other First Division clubs – the two Manchester clubs, Chelsea, Tottenham Hotspur – being interested in me. But that is all it amounted to: talk. I still could not imagine myself going elsewhere in England; I couldn't do that to the West Ham fans.

Tampa were keen for me to go back on a permanent basis; they knew I had enjoyed my short spell. Additionally, the climate was great and Tampa wasn't that far from Bermuda. It meant Kimberley's grandparents would be able to come and visit instead of having to make a round trip of 8,000 miles to see us in the UK.

I made the decision to leave West Ham for good at the end of the 1975/76 season. I was only in my mid-20s and it was a hard decision to make, but I thought I could help to make a difference in the US. If it hadn't been something new, I may have had second thoughts. Some people might say I wasn't mature enough to make a call of such magnitude, but I thought I was. It had to happen sometime and the fact that I knew I had a career to look forward to in the USA made it an easier decision. Any player who plays professional football and is prepared to just sit there, pick up his wages, watch the team struggle – we finished eighteenth again – and not be a part of it has something wrong with his brain. You want to be out there playing. Rather than just stay and suffer, you are better off getting somewhere else.

I will never forget that last day at the club. Ron Greenwood had become general manager, shunted upstairs, as I mentioned earlier. So that's exactly where I headed: upstairs to his office to shake his hand and say goodbye.

I went down to the locker room once again but this time there was not much there. I think I had already given my boots to one of the sixteen-year-old apprentices. I looked round one final time, imagining I might bump into those who had become my best friends over the years: Harry Redknapp, Martin Peters, Geoff Hurst, Bobby Moore; but it was a vain hope. They had all left the club and now it was my turn.

I walked out of the front doors and down the steps to a waiting taxi, turning up the collar of my raincoat, looking out one last time at my surroundings. It was goodbye to the annual Supporters Dance at Stratford Town Hall, goodbye Mama Cass, the restaurant I had frequented, goodbye Lacey's Coaches, goodbye the Black Lion pub and the Baker's Arms, and goodbye the British Legion Band that I loved listening to at half-time.

If there's one thing you can depend on in England it's the weather. Just like the day I arrived at Heathrow as an innocent teenager all those years ago – it seemed like a million years – so mother nature seemed to shed a tear for the Hammer from Bermuda.

It had all happened so quickly, but I was looking at the bigger picture. Obviously I was sad because West Ham had been my life. In football you meet so many wonderful people; it's something I have always appreciated about England. West Ham are an institution. Everyone there is so down to earth. To give you an example, last time I went back, there was a guy in the pub who turned and said to me, 'Hey, Clyde, where you been all these years? On vacation?'

That's what happens in England. Fans stay loyal for life.

But now I was a full-time Tampa player rather than on loan, playing first in the 1976 indoor league – which we won, with me being named Most Valuable Player – then outdoors. Ron Greenwood always used to say that if you were any good, you could play in someone's living room. When I first started at Tampa, we were only playing to around 1,500 spectators. But American sports fans have a winning mentality and in my second season there we were getting around 50,000. I know that sounds an incredible leap but it's the reality. We got the parents interested and, in America, when you get the parents you get the kids. We were entertainers and the public came out in droves to watch. It wasn't just us. The Cosmos were packing them in too.

Having won the Soccer Bowl in my loan season, we got to the semi-finals this time, only to lose to Toronto, who had a certain Eusebio in their ranks. We were holding our own until there were about ten minutes to go when the Black Panther, as he was known, snatched it away from us with two free kicks that he buried. My thoughts were now firmly on remaining in the States, though I have to say it would have been wonderful to have played for West Ham in the 1976 European Cup Winners' Cup final, which unfortunately they lost to Anderlecht. Hey ho . . . you should never look back, and I knew the time was right to move on. Besides, I was playing in the same side as some darned good players – some of those I have already spoken about plus Rodney Marsh. All of us helped put football on the map in the States. It was a privilege being able to play with these guys, many of whom had been household names in their own countries.

Off the pitch, public relations played a massive role, often entailing us agreeing to go to soccer camps to spread the footballing message. The development of the game in the United States may have been behind Europe but they were streets ahead – and still are – when it comes to PR. Yes, we reaped the material benefits off the field, but we couldn't just sit on our laurels. We had to show willing and give something back.

Perhaps the Portland Timbers management had liked what they saw of me when I played against them in the Soccer Bowl because in my second season in Florida I was informed by Tampa that I was being 'traded'. I had only signed for one season, as was usually the case in my career. Yet no sooner had Alfreida, Kimberley and I set foot in Oregon than we found ourselves moving for a few months in the opposite direction – actually 7,000 miles in the opposite direction – back to Europe. Once again we had to check our atlas of Europe to figure out exactly where we were going.

I never intended to go back to Europe but Feyenoord were one of the iconic European clubs. I remember having seen them in the 1974 UEFA Cup final – a big tournament in those days – with the maestro that was Wim van Hanegem in central midfield. They also had a brilliant winger, Jorgen Kristiansen from Denmark. Feyenoord had scouts going backwards and forwards to the States and I just couldn't pass up the chance to play against the likes of Ajax and PSV Eindhoven.

Rotterdam is one of the largest ports in Europe. It sits on the North Sea where the rivers Rhine and Meuse meet. While we were being given a tour of the city after we arrived I wondered why I felt so much at home. In the centre of the city, there seemed to be new construction going on in street after street, with cranes, bulldozers, excavators going full blast. Then our guide explained. Just like the East End of London, the Luftwaffe had flattened the heart of Rotterdam during the Second World War. Thousands of civilians had been killed and many more made homeless. More than thirty years on the city was still being rebuilt.

I felt an instant kinship with the Dutch, who gave my family a lovely welcome. The club found us accommodation in the fashionable Zuiderpark Hotel, where I was warmly greeted by the staff. When we first arrived we were given the luxurious bridal suite.

Feyenoord had just finished fourth in the league, after twelve years of being either champions or runners-up. While it wasn't quite a disaster, they weren't used to being outside the top two and quickly needed to win back the fans and their own self-belief. Their plight wasn't helped by the fact that their talisman Nico Jansen had sustained a broken leg just before the season began; the club's assistant coach, Peter Stephan, had contacted Portland to see if I could go on loan and both clubs agreed terms. Many of Feyenoord's best players, including Wim van Hanegem, had left the club or retired. They wanted me to be the great striker they'd lacked since Sweden's Ove Kindvall, who had famously scored the extra-time winner in the 1970 European Cup final against Celtic.

THE ACID TEST

But it didn't work out. Compared to my time at West Ham, I simply didn't perform. Some of the Dutch media made fun of me, saying that the beard I had grown made me look years older than I really was – 26 when the 1977/78 season started. But I wasn't the only one who performed below par. Feyenoord only managed tenth place in my one season in Rotterdam – a disaster for a club of that stature – but it wasn't fair for me to shoulder all the blame, even though I only scored three goals in 23 appearances, which was admittedly a low return in terms of my expectations.

While I wasn't there long enough to be a success, I honestly had no regrets, though the training was brutal, far harder even than it had been at West Ham – and that was only the morning session. Alfreida was surprised when I didn't come home for lunch, and amazed when I told her about the afternoon sessions.

The coach we had at the time, Vujadin Boskov, ran us into the ground. Twice a day – run, run and run. He was so demanding, but he had a good way about him and you have to remember that training twice a day was the norm in some European countries. Boskov later managed Sampdoria to their first – and so far only – Serie A title and took them to the 1992 European Cup final. These unparalleled heights in the club's history were undoubtedly down to his approach, but I just wasn't used to it and found it very hard.

My fitness improved rapidly and I got off to a really good start when the season actually began, scoring against PSV Eindhoven. My confidence was high and I seemed to be fitting in well. That goal came in my second game in August 1977, but then the goals dried up and I didn't find the net again until November. It was a frustrating time. I was at my physical peak and had shed almost twelve pounds in weight but the goals simply would not come. By mid-season, having been in the top three, everything started to dip.

As I say, I don't regret going there for a single moment. I got really friendly with Ray Clarke, who was at rivals Sparta Rotterdam, having tried out at Tottenham. He never quite made it in north London – I remember once playing against him when in the reserves – but at Sparta Ray was the real deal. He really set them on fire. The point is, Ray was never given a proper opportunity at Spurs. Sparta seemed to feel he would fit instantly into the Dutch game and they were proved right. So much so that he later went on to play in an extremely talented Ajax team before ending his career back in England with Newcastle and going on to become a highly respected scout. You'd have to ask Spurs why they let him go.

I took a lot of positives from my time at Feyenoord. My daughter went to nursery school and ended up speaking Dutch just by playing with the other kids. They would teach her Dutch and she'd teach them English. They'd come round to the house and speak in both languages. When you have these sort of experiences, you really have to take advantage of it.

I'm not trying to make excuses, but I had been playing on Astroturf with Portland during the summer and now I was being asked to make the instant transition back to natural grass in Europe, where everyone had virtually had the summer off. An immediate switch of surface really can make a difference to your form. It worked the other way too while I was at Portland. I'll never forget Manchester United coming over for a friendly. They had Gordon McQueen in central defence, who was not renowned for backing out of tackles. But he brought rubber studs, which you never really played with on Astroturf. You would use a shoe that gripped the surface and prevented you from sliding. While the rest of the guys had proper footwear, poor Gordon just had no control and went sliding all over the place. It was hilarious!

It wasn't only the surface I had problems with, however. I really found it difficult adjusting to the Dutch system of football. In England, and especially at West Ham, I was always supported by two wingers such as Harry Redknapp and Pat Holland. But at Feyenoord I was up against two centre-halves with no support from the flanks. I just couldn't get going.

When Nico Jansen returned from injury the coach played both of us together as a strike force. I laid on a couple of goals for Nico and for a while things looked up again. However, Boskov decided to split us up and my drought continued. Portland Timbers were anxious to have me back in Oregon for the start of the 1978/79 NASL season and, although I reluctantly handed back the new Pontiac that Feyenoord had given me, by April 1978 we were winging our way back Stateside.

19

THE CITY OF ROSES

ONCE AGAIN THE BEST FAMILY WAS HEADING WEST. ALFREIDA and I initially thought Portland was on the Pacific coast, but it's actually seventy miles inland on the Columbia River. When we flew into the airport we were astonished at the beauty of the scenery as the plane swooped over the magnificent Cascade mountain range to the east of the city, with Mount Hood and Mount Rainier towering in the distance.

Portland is known as the City of Roses, due to the climate and the soil. We moved into a beautiful house in the suburb of Tigard, south of Portland and we soon settled Kimberley into a nursery school in the area.

There's something special about Oregon. Not that I didn't enjoy Tampa Bay. I mean, how could you not like playing with Rodney Marsh? Rodney may have had a reputation as a bit of a playboy but he was one of the best players of his era and a gentleman to boot. When I speak about Georgie Best and Pelé, Rodney was not far behind. On his day, he was a magician. I was always amazed at his ball skills for such a big fellow. Plus, he was an extremely intelligent person.

Let me let you into a secret. I was the one who told Tampa about Rodney. He was at Manchester City at the time. I told them I knew of this wonderful, flamboyant player who would bring fans flocking to the stadium. One of the owners of Tampa at the time flew over to see him play against Crystal Palace and was hooked. Within a few days they signed him, much to the frustration of the Cosmos, who were also in for him. Tampa sold him a good package and it worked for both parties. Even today he still lives in the area.

Rodney was a treat to play with – and helped me raise my own standards. He certainly wasn't a troublemaker. In fact, I struggle to recall anyone who brought their club into disrepute throughout my career, though back then we didn't have the same kind of intensive media scrutiny we have now, so scandals were rarely exposed. We didn't have the sort of lurid newspaper headlines we do today, so the relationship between the players and the press was very different. You got to know the people in the news business. Many times after games you'd talk to journalists in the players' lounge or on the train back and you knew they wouldn't stitch you up or try and make stories out of nothing. There was a mutual respect. It's a shame there is so much mistrust today.

Much as I loved Portland, it was a wrench to leave Tampa. I was told much later on that the club regarded letting me and Stewart Scullion go to Oregon as the biggest mistake they ever made. Stewart and I lived on the same complex and got on really well. Last time I spoke to him, he was living in Hampshire. I loved playing with him because his passion for the game, as a wiry little Scotsman, was infectious. We could have built a dynasty in Tampa but Eddie Firmani ultimately thought he could do without us. Once you are a professional footballer, you come to expect this sort of thing to happen. If I'm honest, though, it happened a bit soon for my liking; when I heard Portland were interested, at first I didn't want to go. Life in Florida had been great. Still, Portland is a unique place. I tell people all the time that if they want to raise a family, there aren't many better areas.

The Portland Timbers had been awarded their franchise in 1975, making it to that Soccer Bowl where I helped to beat them. That game endeared the Timbers to the local public and when I started there, attendances averaged about 14,000. That may not seem a lot but they were one of the most passionately followed 'franchises', as Americans insist on calling their clubs.

Despite being 8,000 miles from the East End of London, I still followed the fortunes of West Ham – how could I not? I did my best to get all the results on a Saturday night. But life in Portland was nigh-on perfect and in 1978 we acquired a familiar face as coach when Don Megson was recruited from Bristol Rovers. One of the first signings Don made, to my absolute joy, was to bring in my dearest friend Clive Charles, who by then was playing for Cardiff City having left West Ham. It was fabulous being reunited with Clive.

He was no stranger to the NASL. West Ham had loaned him briefly to Montreal Olympique while he was playing in the reserves. He met his wife Clarena in Montreal and they always planned to return to America at the end of his playing career. When the opportunity to join the Timbers came up, Clive didn't hesitate.

In all I played 124 games for the Timbers over four seasons – with short spells at Feyenoord and Cleveland (indoors) in between – before moving to Toronto and then, finally, to Los Angeles, where I played indoors for the Los Angeles Lazers. As for my old mate Clive, he followed me to the Lazers before going back to Portland to coach, first at high-school level, then at the University of Portland. In 1995 he was appointed as assistant coach on the US men's national team and the following year he became head coach of the US men's Olympic soccer team. One of the highlights for him must surely have been the 3–0 win over Canada in 1997 in Vancouver that qualified the USA for the World Cup in France the following year. What a guy. A class act, great friend and excellent family man. I still miss him dearly.

BRIAN TILER, ONE OF HARRY REDKNAPP'S CLOSEST FRIENDS, WAS the person who lured me and Stewart Scullion, a firecracker of a player, to Portland where he had taken over as coach. After a short while, Brian went back to England, where he became managing director of Bournemouth and helped mastermind their first ever promotion to the old Second Division. Brian's death in 1990 was a terrible tragedy. He was killed in a road accident when a car smashed head-on into the minibus in which he and Harry were travelling during the World Cup in Italy. Harry was badly injured, but survived and went on to make a full recovery. We used to call Brian 'Toby' and I was completely devastated, as were all the Portland players – and, I imagine, all the other clubs Toby had association with. He was a fantastic human being.

After Toby left Portland, we brought in Don Megson and after him Vic Crowe returned as head coach, having served in that capacity when the club was formed. At the time, Portland didn't have an indoor team but Cleveland did, and that's where I was off to next with the family.

Way back in the early 1970s I remember having great battles with Mike England when we played Spurs. As centre-halves go, Mike was among the most uncompromising you could get, though he always played fair. After one particular encounter, as I was about to get up to leave the players' lounge, Mike looked across and shouted, 'Best of luck, see you next time.' As you do.

It never occurred to me that this 'next time' would take place on the other side of the world. But that's exactly what happened. When I went to play indoors for Cleveland Force, one of the six charter franchises in the original Major Indoor Soccer League (MISL), who should I discover had also signed than Mike, who had previously been with the Seattle Sounders.

The coach was Eddie McCreadie, the former Chelsea stalwart. Again I was in the company of one of the best people I ever met in football. Eddie was a diamond. He was down to earth, listened to his players and was not at all big-headed. But there was another, even greater Chelsea legend on the playing staff. Alan Hudson was an unbelievable player. I would put him and Charlie George in same bracket. Huddy could make a soccer ball talk. It's unfortunate that he never really got the England caps he deserved to go with his supreme ability.

Cleveland played at the Richfield Coliseum, home of the Cleveland Cavaliers, the city's basketball team, and regularly drew crowds of over 10,000, many of whom had come to see Huddy, surely one of the most gifted midfielders of his generation. Our nickname was inspired by 'The Force', a mystical power used by the Jedi Knights in the movie *Star Wars*. Often us ex-pats would all just sit around reminiscing about games we had played against each other. One day one of them mentioned that he had heard Trevor Brooking had scored a goal with his head. We all fell about laughing. A Trevor header? Not possible! In all the games I played with Trevor I had seen him score lots of beautiful goals – but never with his head. Of course, a few weeks later Trevor scored the winning goal for West Ham in the FA Cup final against Arsenal – with his head!

In all I played 30 games for Cleveland, scoring 33 goals, with 16 assists. I was voted onto the MISL All-Star Squad, a nice way of remembering my short time there. In those days you were allowed to switch from the outdoor league to the indoor league and back again with different teams.

It wasn't hard going back to Portland; it's still one of my favourite cities, full of great people who loved us to death. But my time there was running out. After one particular game against Vancouver Whitecaps, I remember Vic Crowe telling me that my performance made me his 'number one man'. Coaches say lots of things when they want to sell something to you. In summer 1980 I took sick like never before when I contracted diverticulitis caused by a cyst on my intestine. It was serious stuff but, thank goodness, not cancerous. Nevertheless, I was out for around five months, the longest layoff of my career. It was really tough but I couldn't rush myself back and had to listen to the doctors. When I had recovered and got back in time for the following indoor season (by then Portland also had an indoor team), there was suddenly no place for me even though I was supposed to be the 'number one man'. I told myself if that was the case, then maybe I was better moving on. Throughout my career I was usually the one who instigated moving. That was a good thing: I was more or less in charge of my own destiny. It's far worse when someone comes and tells you it's time to pack up.

Attendances in Portland had been falling because there was a lot of uncertainty about the future of the league. Plus, results were not great. Having twice missed out on the playoffs, we did manage to get to what by then was known as the Conference Final in 1978, but we lost to the New York Cosmos. The team eventually folded at the end of the 1982 season as player salaries outpaced revenue, but the Timbers' legacy lives on. That area of the country is still mad about the round-ball game. I'd like to think I contributed to that.

While I was with Portland, I had the good fortune to be invited as a guest player with the Los Angeles Aztecs, who had signed Johan Cruyff. He may no longer have been in his heyday but he was still a mesmerising talent. When he ran at people they had no idea which way he was going to go. Like George Best and Pelé, Cruyff had everything. He could dribble, pass, head, tackle, defend and score goals. When I toured with Cruyff and the Aztecs in October 1979, we visited his native Holland, France and England. Obviously I was keen to prove to the fans in both countries where I had played league football that I could still do the business. We had an up-and-down few games in Holland, then drew 1–1 with Birmingham City before going down 2–0 at Chelsea. The highlight was a 2–1 win against Paris St-Germain. When we were awarded a penalty, which I actually won, I automatically assumed Cruyff would take it, but he asked me to instead. I thought that was an amazing gesture for one of the most revered players in the world. Not only that. All through the match, he had been picking me out from fifty yards, right on my chest. I couldn't believe the vision, even though he was in his thirties by then.

His death in March 2016 from cancer shocked the world and it's easy to understand why. It wasn't only on the pitch that Cruyff excelled. He took stardom in his stride. When it came to the everyday person, he was a very humble guy. Yes, he could be hard on his players at times when he became a coach, but he was always honest.

It was really satisfying that a team of supposed has-beens could compete with top-level European clubs. Rinus Michels, the great Dutch coach credited with the concept of 'total football', was the Aztecs coach at that time and to work with one of game's greatest ever philosophers was an extraordinary turn of good fortune. Rinus was affectionately known as 'the General' or 'the Sphinx' because of his stern manner on the field, but off it he was a warm and humorous character. As innovative as he was inspirational, Rinus loved working with skilful players but he also always encouraged those who might not have been blessed with as much ability as others – provided they gave their full effort all of the time.

When Rinus died in 2005, I remember Cruyff saying he would not have become the player he was without the help of the General. 'There is nobody who taught me as much as him,' Johan said at the time. Scores of others must have felt the same way.

WINDING DOWN FROM EAST TO WEST

BY 1981 IT HAD BECOME CLEAR I WAS NO LONGER GUARANTEED first-team football at Portland. It was then that I got wind of the fact Toronto Blizzard were interested in signing me. Being something of a nomad, I decided to take a chance and move over the border into Canada, albeit only for one season. When I arrived I again saw a host of familiar faces, including Jim Bone (Norwich City, Sheffield United, Partick Thistle), Jimmy Greenhoff (Leeds United, Birmingham City, Stoke City, Manchester United, Crewe Alexandra and Port Vale) and the great Peter Lorimer (Leeds United). I remembered Jimmy well after those heavyweight clashes against Stoke and we established an instant rapport. In my very first game for Toronto, I set up two goals for him against Fort Lauderdale Strikers, a game we won 3–1.

I enjoyed working with Blizzards coach Clive Toye. He impressed me with his coaching methods and knowledge and I admired him hugely. Not many journalists become senior coaches but Clive was one. A lifelong Exeter City fan, he had made his name as a sports writer with the *Daily Express* before going to live in the States, where he helped bring the NASL to fruition and became best known as the man who tempted Pelé to join the New York Cosmos in 1975 and, in a sense, changed the course of American soccer history. Pelé's contract with Santos in his native Brazil had finally run out and he was being courted by Juventus and Real Madrid. Clive, using all the persuasive skills gleaned from a career in journalism, persuaded Pelé that if he went to the USA he would win over an entire nation.

As I did at every club I played for, I gave my all in every game for Toronto. It was nice to know I hadn't been forgotten but there were a number of upheavals, especially at management level. As an area and an environment, though, I loved it. Toronto has so many people of different ethnic backgrounds. Camaraderie in the team was high but as I was getting older so I struggled with little niggles. Additionally, I just couldn't get used to the freezing temperatures. Even in spring and summer when the sun shone during the day, the thermometer seemed to drop to zero in the evening. Environment isn't only about weather, of course. I loved the city and Lake Ontario but I'm just not a cold-weather guy. I did my best for the team but eight wins and ten defeats in the American Conference, Eastern Division, that season wasn't ideal, even though I felt I managed to steady the ship.

Twelve months later it didn't take much to persuade me to move from Toronto to Los Angeles – especially when the person trying to lure me there was Clive Charles. Clive was coaching the Lazers and called to ask if I would be interested in joining. I didn't think twice. After all, we had grown up together and we had a telepathic understanding both on the field and off. Besides, I sensed that this might prove to be the last hurrah in my long professional career.

The Major Indoor Soccer League had awarded a Los Angeles franchise to Jerry Buss in June 1982. Buss had purchased the Philadelphia Fever and wanted to move it to California. After receiving approval, he renamed the team the Los Angeles Lazers. Jerry also owned the Los Angeles Lakers of the National Basketball Association and the name was deliberately created to give it a firm association with the famous basketball team.

The Lazers played their home games in the Forum in Inglewood, California. The stadium had a capacity of about 15,000 but we only ever had one third of that number watching us – the sort of crowd you'd get in the lower reaches of the English football pyramid. At the time, LA being the city it was, indoor football was new to them. In the States, you have to show the people what your intentions are. Once they find out that they are good, they'll support you.

I was proud of what I'd achieved in the States. When I started there, the sport was still struggling to find its place. It's a sad coincidence that when I stopped playing in 1984, the NASL collapsed. That's what happens when you don't get your finances right. Let's face it, there are clubs in England even today who go into receivership. Although the NASL ultimately failed, it introduced soccer to the North American sports scene on a large scale for the first time, and was a major contributing factor in the sport becoming massively popular among American youth. I also believe the NASL provided lessons for its successor, Major League Soccer, which took all the right precautions against such problems.

People often downplay how much America has contributed to the world game. The country has created a lot of trends that Europe took up only later. Just the other night I was watching television back home in Bermuda and realised how things that started in the States – like cheerleaders and names on the back of shirts – had been part of their culture for ages. The Americans are brilliant at marketing and selling a product. I had little doubt football would take off there in the way it did.

WHEN IT WAS FINALLY TIME TO CALL IT A DAY, ALFREIDA AND I opened a dry-cleaning business in Irvine, California. That may sound a strange thing to do but when I lived in England, I always remembered the phrase, 'Where there's muck, there's money,' meaning where there are dirty jobs to be done, there is often money to be made. Alfreida and I bought the business from a friend, called it Quality Cleaning, and took on eight staff. I wanted to prove to myself as much as to other people that I could do something outside of football. It was nice striking up relationships with ordinary folk. Once you hang those boots up, you have to do something.

I also started dabbling in coaching, first at high-school level, then at Irvine Valley Junior College, where we won the California State championship – a great achievement for myself and the youngsters involved. One of them I worked with was Joe-Max Moore, who went on to win more than 100 caps with the United States national team. I always had an idea Joe would make the grade and, sure enough, he did very well both in Germany and England, where he spent three years at Everton. It was great helping a young player like him to develop

I always believed it would only be a matter of time before the United States had a team that could become a power in world football. Not only was it the sheer number of youngsters available but also their attitude – attentive, keen to learn, enthusiastic and hard-working. It helped that America has excellent sports facilities. Their national association provides a strong framework to give players the chance to work their way through the junior ranks and into the senior team.

By the mid-1990s I was actually coaching about ten different age groups and loving every minute of it. Irvine is a beautiful area to raise a family, just south of Los Angeles close to the magnificent state parks of Crystal Cove and Canyon View. We had a lovely home, we worked hard and my coaching skills were sought after and appreciated by the different schools and colleges.

The reason I never made a career of coaching at the highest level was nothing to do my colour, more the fact that I don't think I could have handled the way so many professional players behave. That's why I concentrated on helping younger ones – the exception being my own national team. Let's face it, many senior pros are so spoilt and like to have their own way. Money can go to your head when you are earning millions of dollars a year. When I played, if you acted up you got slapped down. From what I hear, a lot of today's elite footballers, if they don't like what they are being told, just decide to leave. Coaching big-name players just wasn't for me. Yet I'm disturbed about how few black coaches there are in the game, even today. It's something I frequently get asked about. Is it latent racism? Is it because owners and chairman naively believe we aren't cut out for it? A few years back, remember, people used to say black players couldn't handle the cold. How ridiculous. Look at the number of black players in England, and all over western Europe, at the present time. There are more black players than white in some teams. So that's one myth cast out the window.

We do have to find a way to clear up this black manager thing. Why are we still discussing the same issue we were discussing when I was playing? There are loads of black guys out there who, if given the opportunity, would do a good job. You just have to make sure they are given the opportunity. Jimmy Floyd Hasselbaink, who has just gone to Queens Park Rangers, needs to be given time; though how ironic that he took over from one of the few other black managers in the country, Chris Ramsey.

It grieves me that they are so few and far between. Surely you shouldn't have to look at the colour of a person's skin to see if they are able to coach. If a black player has been at your club since his youth and has worked his way up, why not take a gamble on him to be the coach? From what I hear, Chris Ramsey was instrumental in Harry Kane's development at Spurs. You're not going to tell me that he can't evaluate players and put them through the system. Owners and chairman have to be willing to sit around the table and say, 'Hey, let's make sure we take these guys on.' Over the years, there has been the occasional black manager in the Netherlands such as Frank Rijkaard and in England with the likes of Ruud Gullit and Chris Hughton, but very few European countries have followed suit. It won't happen overnight but we have to be more inclusive.

In the States, they have the Rooney rule, which has worked well. For those of you unfamiliar with the rule, it has nothing to do with Wayne Rooney! In essence, it requires America's National Football League teams (that's gridiron) to interview at least one minority candidate for head coaching and other senior jobs. The rule is named after Dan Rooney, the owner of Pittsburgh Steelers who has long given African-Americans leadership roles. It was created in 2002 after head coaches Tony Dungy of the Tampa Bay Buccaneers and Dennis Green of the Minnesota Vikings were fired, even though Dungy had a winning record and Green had just had his first losing season in ten years.

Since the Rooney Rule was established, several NFL franchises have hired non-white head coaches. At the start of the 2006 season, the overall percentage of African-American coaches had jumped to 22 per cent, up from 6 per cent prior to the rule being introduced. They realised in the States there was a problem and did something quite simple and straightforward, very easy to implement, that also produced lasting results. Yet in England, everyone seems to be running away from it.

21

TIME TO GO HOME

IN THE AUTUMN OF 1996 I RECEIVED A LONG-DISTANCE PHONE call from Bermuda. It was from the Bermuda Football Association asking if I would be interested in taking on the role of technical director. With my experience of playing in two continents and coaching in one, I was well qualified to take on the role. The appointment would be an interim one of six months from the following January through to June. Hopefully, I thought, I could make it permanent after that, maybe with a three-year contract.

I had a lot of thinking to do. By that time Kimberley was studying English at Messiah College on the other side of the United States in Pennsylvania, Alfreida and I were running a successful business, we were respected in the community and had put down roots in the area.

I am, however, Bermudian through and through. My heart will always be there and I had to put my country first. Alfreida, Kimberley and I talked at length about the offer and arrived at a decision. Almost three decades after first boarding that flight to London and playing with and against some of the most famous players on the planet, after a career that had taken me from obscurity to the best league and the best club in the world for eight years, and then across the Atlantic to rub shoulders with the likes of Pelé and Franz Beckenbauer, I was going home. And I decided that it would be for good.

The BFA had actually invited me to take a couple of coaching workshops with some of the kids the year before offering me a full-time post and, I assumed, liked what they had seen and felt I could do a good job as national coach / technical director, call it what you will. Effectively I had to do both jobs.

Apart from my own belief in myself, two factors gave me high hopes that I could be successful. One was my own memories of growing up among an array of talented players, several of whom went on to play professionally overseas despite our tiny population. I believe that was down to sheer passion and the readiness to train hard. Sometimes we had to walk miles just to get to training.

The second encouraging factor was that the Bermuda national team had acquitted itself well in the CONCACAF World Cup qualifying campaign for the 1994 finals, which suggested that there was great potential. That team included two promising young forwards, Shaun Goater, then a 21-year-old starting his professional career with Rotherham United in England, and Kyle Lightbourne, who went on to play for Walsall and Stoke City among other clubs. Bermuda had managed victories over Haiti, Antigua and, most notably, El Salvador during that campaign, as well as getting draws against Jamaica and Canada. That may not sound particularly impressive to an England or Brazil fan, but for such a tiny island those results meant we were really punching above our weight.

I was happy to have Gary Darrell working as my assistant. Gary had played in the NASL with the Washington Diplomats and also alongside me in the Bermuda national team. My first major tournament was confirmed as the Caribbean Cup in Jamaica in 1998, so we should have had plenty of time to prepare. The early signs were promising. The 25 players we wanted to have a look at turned out for an initial training session in the rain the day after the New Year's Day holiday. There seemed to be plenty of desire as we outlined to them that we were serious about our plans for a progressive national programme and that there would be more to keep them interested than simply a jolly.

I became even more enthused about the future when the BFA unveiled its six-year plan at a press conference: it would cost around $4 million and would involve the island sending teams of various levels into seven international competitions over the following three years. The plan included scope for six senior-level international matches in Bermuda each year as well as two overseas tournaments. This was important to me, as I knew that if our amateur players were going to make any progress we would need regular international exposure. That can be an expensive venture when living on an isolated island with the nearest land mass around 600 miles away. It sounded like my employers were offering the earth. It didn't quite pan out that way.

Our two games against a Jamaica side which was on the way to qualifying for the 1998 World Cup in France showed me how far we had to go. We lost both narrowly, 1–0 and 3–2, but it was clear that our players needed to get fitter and tougher to compete at that level. The reality was that the 'Reggae Boyz' had enjoyed good financial support from their government and they'd been boosted by a recent tour of Europe and a training camp in Argentina. That sort of thing was pie in the sky to us. Most of our players only had experience of playing in the Bermuda league, so this introduction to international football was understandably a shock to the system. But Jamaica were an example to us of what a small island could achieve in football, given the necessary resources.

I wanted to start at school level and build upwards from there, getting some of our top coaches involved. Too often these days, coaches of young teams can spoil a youngster's development by placing too much emphasis on winning and not enough time on learning skills and simply having fun. Winning matches should not be the most important priority for an under-10 team, but you would never think that, listening to some of the people who coach them. Pressuring such young kids to get results is ridiculous, not to mention counter-productive.

I therefore set up four Schools of Excellence across the island to try to spread the message that the basic skills were what kids needed to learn. Each youngster was also taught a 'player's creed', a copy of which was also given to parents. This allowed the children to know precisely what was expected of them in terms of standards of behaviour, and it was designed to introduce their young minds to the idea that being a sportsman is about much more than just playing the game.

I also hired a head coach, Robert Calderon, to work with me. Highly respected in Bermuda footballing circles, he was a former national team player who had enjoyed plenty of local success. The next problem was how to find suitable opponents. Remember, Bermuda is a two-hour flight off the US mainland. It wasn't as if I could just call up some other national coach and say, 'Can you bring your team over next week for a friendly match?'

As we headed for the Cayman Islands for Caribbean Cup qualifier games in May 1998, we managed to secure en route a useful friendly against US Major League Soccer team Miami Fusion at their stadium in Fort Lauderdale. Miami had Colombian World Cup star Carlos Valderrama in their ranks and he scored a typically classy goal, side-stepping a defender and then feigning to commit our goalkeeper Timmy Figureido, before rolling his shot just inside the post. The second half was delayed by a massive thunderstorm and accompanying downpour, and within minutes of the restart we were down 2–0, thanks to a deflected free kick.

My heart burst with pride as I watched our young, mostly amateur, team come back to win. Paul Cann pulled one back with a volley after which I made a triple substitution to give three of our youngsters – Damon Ming, Tafari Outerbridge and Reggie Tucker – a chance to show what they could do. The response was superb and David Bascome scored a brace to give us an unlikely 3–2 victory.

We got a massive boost in confidence from the result and really looked forward to the upcoming games against the Cayman Islands and Cuba. However, it was to prove a disappointment. We hit problems almost as soon as we landed in Grand Cayman. The Cayman Islands FA had promised us training facilities but they let us down big time as there was no field available. Eventually we found a patch of grass – a makeshift cricket field – where we were able to do some light work. It was far from ideal, as it was situated at the junction of two roads, where a lot of balls ended up. To make matters worse, when we got back to the hotel to eat, the establishment had run out of food, so the players ended up having to stuff themselves with potato crisps, chocolate bars and soda for nutrition. You couldn't make it up. Well actually, you could, given the scandalous facilities in the region which I earlier alluded to. I don't believe I bore any responsibility for this incident as coach. How was I supposed to know?

Cuba and the Caymans drew the opening match in our qualification group 2–2, before we came up against the Cubans in our first test. We lost 2–1 but had to play nearly the whole of the second half with ten men after Dennis Robinson was sent off for a rather mysterious second yellow card. Even more disappointing was our 2–0 defeat to the Caymans, a team we would normally have expected to beat and one of the few countries with a population smaller than Bermuda's! In both matches, missed chances cost us dear.

That experience underlined the value of match practice. Cuba had played eight matches in the run-up to the tournament and the Caymans four, while we had squeezed in one friendly on the way to the event. I did not want to take a

Bermuda team into international competition so short of match practice again.

Organisation and officiating seemed to be problematic all over the region – and still are. CONCACAF have a lot to learn when it comes to proper distribution of resources. It's a complete joke the way the confederation keeps imploding. First the Jack Warner era, then Jeff Webb. Neither of them seemed to have the interests of the smaller regions of the continent at heart yet they were both from the Caribbean. Webb is even from the Cayman Islands, yet all either of these two gentlemen were seemingly interested in was lining their pockets.

When I took the team to Antigua for a World Cup tie, it got even worse. We were given a cow field to train on. I kid you not. I just can't get my head round the appalling way wealth has been distributed – or hasn't – around our region. It's disgraceful. Even today, so many footballers in the region don't know where their next meal is coming from

CONCACAF's role is supposed to be to make sure all the countries in the region are developed properly and, as far as I can see, that hasn't happened, especially when you look at all the funds supposedly dished out. Everybody in the region should have decent pitches, not just one or two countries. Jack Warner, as I've said before, needs to take a lot of responsibility for this.

THE MOST APPALLING REFEREEING I HAVE EVER WITNESSED WAS also in the Caribbean, when I took a Bermuda under-21 team to St Kitts and Nevis in 1998. It was a qualifier for a regional CONCACAF tournament and we had drawn our first match 2–2 with Barbados, which left us needing to beat the host nation by two clear goals to progress to the finals, to be staged in Venezuela. We comprehensively outplayed St Kitts, but lost 2–1, due largely to the fact that we had no fewer than *four* goals disallowed. All of them came from corners and I have no idea why the Guyanese referee chalked off any of them. You can't be offside from a corner, yet that's what happened to us. It was robbery. It wasn't fair on the players, who gave their all and deserved to qualify. They were gutted. I can't prove it but I'm pretty certain match-fixing was involved at some level. It wasn't a crime you heard much about back then, not like now, and no one had any hard evidence. But it does make you wonder. Nothing surprises me in this region.

*

I FELT THAT WE WERE MAKING STEADY PROGRESS AS A FOOTBALL nation. In 1999 Bermuda staged a Caribbean Cup qualifying tournament in which we thrashed the Bahamas 6–0 and walloped the Cayman Islands 4–1, before we went down 2–1 to a talented Cuban side, many of whom played for the same professional club side in Germany.

Better still, our team of construction workers, teachers, bankers and so on managed to register a 2–0 win against a visiting Denmark under-23 team. Denmark had reached the quarter-finals of the 1998 World Cup and were a real footballing force at the time. Our lads worked tremendously hard and we employed a wing-back system that worked a treat.

But what had really given me a glimpse of a bright future was our under-15 team. I really believed this bunch of talented youngsters had what it took to become a force, at least in the Caribbean region. They had beaten St Vincent over two legs to win a CONCACAF tournament in Trinidad, where they hammered the host nation 3–0 with a stunning display. I was really proud of all of them.

Our first World Cup preliminary-round match was against the British Virgin Islands (BVI) and would take place in March 2000. A month before the first leg I was able to take most of the younger players on a Florida tour so that we at least had some preparation. We were also able to recruit our two England-based professionals, Kyle Lightbourne and Shaun Goater, who was then the top scorer with Manchester City and had assumed cult status. Additionally, we had David Bascome, who by now was playing indoors in the USA with the Harrisburg Heat.

On arrival, it certainly didn't feel like the most important game since I had taken over. The pitch in the capital, Road Town (seriously, that's its name), was rock hard and very uneven. It's no wonder, really, as the field was open to the public. How ridiculous can you get? See what I mean about atrocious facilities? The night before, kids were playing football and cricket all over it under floodlights!

Even though we had Kentoine Jennings sent off inside the first ten minutes, we strolled to a 5–1 victory, with Shaun scoring a hat-trick. For the second leg, a week later at our own Bermuda National Sports Centre, we did not bother to call up Shaun, Kyle and David. Even without them we walloped the BVI 9–0 for a 14–1 aggregate victory.

The next straight knockout qualifier was an altogether tougher affair against Antigua, an island with a similar-sized population to ours. It was the second of three home-and-away rounds before the group stage. We went down there and managed to get a creditable 0–0 draw in St John's. Hopes were high that we would finish the job in Bermuda. But we were without both Kyle and Shaun. Kyle wanted to take his one and only chance to play at Wembley, as Stoke City had made it to the Auto Windscreens Shield final. Shaun had written to the BFA and requested that he not be called up as his club games were a priority. I have mixed feelings about club versus country – always have had. I know clubs pay the players' salaries but I've always thought representing your country was the pinnacle, especially in a World Cup game. Kyle called me from the UK and said that he was very keen to play in the second leg after the final but that his manager Gudjon Thordrason wasn't because it would mean him missing two games in the Easter programme. To add to our woes, David Bascome was injured, so that meant we had none of our three professionals.

We were the better team throughout the return but were wasteful in front of goal. Our captain Shannon Burgess put us ahead from the penalty spot in the second half, but a late equaliser from Antigua gave them a 1–1 draw – and Bermuda was therefore eliminated on the 'away goals' rule.

The teenage strikers we selected played really well and I was proud of them but they did not have the experience to make the most of our chances. If Shaun and Kyle had been playing it would have been a different story.

I was told privately that there had been club pressure on Shaun since he was Manchester City's leading scorer and they were pushing for promotion to the Premier League. His manager, Joe Royle, when the question of Shaun playing for Bermuda came up, was quoted as saying: 'It's not as if Bermuda is going to win the World Cup, is it?'

I have the greatest respect for Big Joe, who was one of the best centre-forwards around when I was playing, and a terrific guy as well. However, I found such comments pretty patronising to say the least. If smaller countries cannot put out their strongest teams in the World Cup, then it degrades the greatest competition in the world. Let's face it, if the same argument was applied across the board, then maybe only a handful of countries would ever play with full-strength teams. The fact is that entering the World Cup is a wasted exercise if you are going to be without your best players for your most important matches. Can you imagine what the reaction would be if World Cup qualification were on the line for England but Roy Hodgson, or whoever the manager was, couldn't select his main weapons because their clubs did not want them to risk getting injured? There would be an outcry.

I will always be grateful that I was given the chance to pass on my skills and experience to a whole generation of Bermuda youngsters as national coach. We had some great times together and to a large extent I have West Ham to thank for all that I learned at Chadwell Heath. My contract with the BFA had been for three years and that was enough for me. It would be fair to say it didn't quite go according to plan and that I got disillusioned. We never got all those promises about international exposure fulfilled. As ever, financial constraints came into play. If you haven't got the money you can't get the experience. I tell people all the time that you can have all the coaching you want but if you don't play matches – meaningful matches against challenging opposition – you're not going to be able to raise your game and improve.

It wasn't easy coaching amateurs. I had to keep reminding myself they all had jobs. It's not like being a professional when everything is done for you. You wake up in the morning, go to training, your kit is there waiting, you just put it on and drop it off.

People often ask me why I never committed myself to coaching. I guess the answer is I never felt totally comfortable with it. Nor was it something I set out to do. That's not to say I don't applaud those who make a career out of it. But it's not an easy profession. Being judged only by results is a tough business.

22

BOLEYN TO STRATFORD

MY OVERRIDING FEELING AS I LOOK BACK AT MY CAREER IS THAT I have done what my father had always urged me to do: given something back to the community that nurtured me and been an example to others. Nobody knew me from Adam when I started out and I'll always be grateful to West Ham for giving me a fair crack.

In 2006, I had the privilege of being awarded an MBE for services to football and the community in Bermuda. I came over with my wife, daughter and one of my sisters to receive the award from Prince Charles, who really put me at ease with his humour. Determined to look the part, I decided before the ceremony to buy a top hat. Well actually, if truth be told, it was Alfreida's idea. There was a swish London outfitters close to where we were staying in central London so in we went, searched for the right hat and then got one mighty shock when we discovered it cost £500. Too much, I protested. I didn't really want to wear it anyway. Nonsense, my dear beloved insisted. So, obviously, I forked out the dough. It cost me a small fortune. But that wasn't the end of it. Oh no. When we got to Buckingham Palace for the investiture, they only went and confiscated the hat for security reasons. No sooner had we got out of the taxi at the gates of Buckingham Palace than an official promptly informed us the hat would have to be collected afterwards. I had to follow protocol. I've still got the wretched thing in its original box back home in Bermuda. I've never worn it. Anyone out there want to buy it?

In all seriousness, you have to remain level-headed after such an honour, which I hope I did. When the Lord calls me home, I'll probably donate it to Somerset Village, where I learned both football and cricket, or maybe bequeath it to West Ham.

Of course there are things I haven't done, like play in the World Cup. But let me make one thing clear as far as international football is concerned. Wikipedia may say I only played a couple of senior games for my country, but it was far more than that. Definitely double figures. If you ask me why it was not dozens of games, it's very simple: we never had that many fixtures. As I have said, we just don't have the funding where I come from. Football is part-time in Bermuda. If I was from somewhere else, maybe I'd have done more on the international stage, but you can't go through life thinking like that. Look at my namesake George Best. He never played in the World Cup either. Many others are in the same boat. Only a select few are blessed to have been able to do that.

It's vitally important when footballers retire that they have something mean-ingful to occupy their time. Those that don't often find it difficult to adapt to everyday life. Paul Gascoigne, a wonderfully gifted player, is a case in point. Paul has had to fight off any number of demons but he is not alone. I have nothing but admiration for ex-players who struggle after hanging up their boots but somehow manage to come out the other side. Sadly, not all of them do. The press should leave them alone and let them be instead of hounding them when things go wrong. I'd put Alan Hudson in the same category. Alan was a fantastic player. Had he somehow managed to stay in the game afterwards, it may have changed a lot of the habits that he had. He's a fantastic human being and we became good friends when I was in the States; he's a really likable person.

I was never going to find myself in that kind of situation, not after what my father had taught me. People do all kinds of things when they quit the game but I wanted to try and make a difference so I worked for around twelve years at Bermuda's Westgate Correctional Centre, the island's main prison. I was employed in the halfway-house section of the building, specifically for prisoners being rehabilitated back into society. Part of my job was to help the inmates understand that nothing in life is easy and that you have to work for what you want. We taught them how to apply for jobs, how to fill out forms, how to cook, stuff like that. In other words, equip them for when they got out. If prisoners are not rehabilitated properly, they are likely to reoffend and go straight back to jail. We didn't have many murders but there was a big drugs problem and it was my job to work with the prisoners before they were released. I treated them in a way I would have wanted to be treated. It certainly helped having played sport because a lot of scenarios you go through relate to everyday life. Our government had a contract with a company from Philadelphia who took me on. The contract eventually ended but I enjoyed every minute. It's very heart-warming to have people coming up to me in the street, even today, thanking me for helping them get through life. I'm a pretty humble guy anyway but it makes me feel even more humble.

Nowadays, I do a radio show once a week on Mondays, talking about sport (naturally). It covers whatever is going on at the time. I also own a fast-food restaurant, Big Eats, which is primarily for prison officers but also for members of the public and opens five days a week selling hamburgers, fish and chips and the like. Apart from that, I watch as much football as I can. With the advent of satellite TV, I am able to catch virtually any fixture I want from the Premier League and, of course, make sure I hardly miss a West Ham game. It's good to see the club thriving under Slaven Bilic, who was a legend in his playing days at Upton Park. Of the current squad, I really hope they can hang on to Dimitri Payet. I love his silky skills. He reminds me of some of those great Brazilians. It's a steal what we bought him for. Andy Carroll has had a hard time through injury. He'd have been great in my day putting away some of those crosses.

By the time you read this, the club will be residing in the Olympic Stadium in Stratford. To be perfectly honest, I have mixed feelings about this. I know it's a symbol of the modern age that clubs have to either expand or build new grounds to maximise their commercial potential. I'm sure it will have been a sad day leaving Upton Park. It's a place full of history and in England we don't destroy our history. There will be a lot of disappointed fans, no doubt. But just as many will relish the move. From a business point of view, on balance it's probably a good idea because more fans through the turnstiles means more revenue to compete in the transfer market. West Ham can't do that where they are now while others can cram in 50,000 or 60,000. Hopefully being at the Olympic Stadium can attract more crowds and, in turn, better players; adding another 20,000 to the gate could push us right up among the elite.

But one man who won't be there to enjoy it is Sam Allardyce. I felt sorry for Big Sam when he was shown the door. I can't say I was really surprised because in one sense he was doomed from the start as a result of his preferred style of play. West Ham is known for trying to play attractive football and keeping it on the ground. If you don't do that, you're going to get slaughtered. That's what happened with Sam, especially in the second part of his final season. He only won two games, which simply wasn't good enough. If he had been at a European club, he probably wouldn't have been allowed to stay as long as he did. West Ham don't sack managers that easily. Luckily we survived that season because of our form in the first half of the campaign. You can't just blame Sam, because the players have to bear some responsibility. But he will have known when he went into West Ham that it's a results-driven business. Which, as I've said before, is one reason why I never fancied it after my playing days.

I shall certainly make a point of coming over and seeing us play at the new ground. The East End will always have a special place in my heart. Such genuine people. The friends I met there will always stay with me, and I'd like to think I treated them all decently. There's nothing wrong with being nice and being polite; it was the way I was brought up.

In the meantime, I'm enjoying my retirement doing some fitness work. It may sound boring but my other hobbies are other sports – cricket, as you know, tennis, and I love fishing. I always did, even from a young age. Getting on a boat and throwing a line over the side is my ideal way of relaxing. I also used to write a regular column for our local newspaper, the *Royal Gazette*.

Whenever I switch on TV to watch games, it gives me so much pleasure seeing so many black players strutting their stuff. What a far cry from when I started out. It's so rewarding that black players have become the norm in so many leagues. If I helped bring that about in some small way, that's good enough for me. All I wanted to do was be a beacon of dignity, to carry the torch a certain way so that fans of every generation could see black players were no different to anyone else.

More often than not these days, you'll find me sitting in an armchair waiting for a match to start. And when that happens, my thoughts invariably hark back to my heyday: perhaps standing in the tunnel at the Boleyn Ground on a rainy winter's day with puddles forming on the pitch. Our opponents are Manchester

United. Their players have just been called from the away dressing room and they file out quietly. The ground is packed to the rafters, with thousands outside unable to gain admission. The rain lashes down on the stands.

We stand in two parallel lines and listen as the public address system comes to life and the announcer in his thick London accent welcomes our opponents to Upton Park. He starts to read out the team sheets. As each Manchester United name is announced we hear massive cheering from the away end. They have brought almost 8,000 supporters. 'Alex Stepney, Paul Edwards, Tony Dunne, Francis Burns, Ian Ure, Pat Crerand, Willie Morgan, Brian Kidd, Bobby Charlton, Denis Law, George Best.'

I glance across. Best and Law, legends both, are right next to me. They stare straight ahead, keeping their concentration. They know they are going to have a battle on their hands today. The announcer carries on: 'This is the West Ham team. Bobby Ferguson, Billy Bonds, Bobby Howe, Martin Peters, Alan Stephenson, Bobby Moore, Harry Redknapp, Jim Lindsay, Geoff Hurst, Peter Eustace, Clyde Best.'

Bobby Moore glances round quickly as if he is just checking to make sure we are all in place. The roars from the crowd reach a crescendo. Once a Hammer, always a Hammer.

POSTSCRIPT

I STARTED MY STORY WITH A CHILLING ACCOUNT OF HOW AN anonymous fan, if you can call him that, sent me a letter threatening to throw acid at me just because of the colour of my skin. But I'd like to end on a more positive note – after all, I like to think I've remained a positive person throughout my life, someone who sees the best in people, even during the toughest times of my playing career.

I believe that people's attitudes can change, are changing, and this was brought home to me when I received a letter of a very different nature a few years ago.

It was from an Englishman who came to Bermuda and became a policeman. I don't know which team he supported but he wanted to apologise for all those occasions when he had hurled insults and abuse from the terraces aimed at me and other black players. He ended up coming to my house to say sorry in person and I accepted his apology. For me, it was great that someone had the courage to front up and recognise that what they had done was wrong.

His remorse showed me that, although it is by no means a thing of the past, racism and prejudice can be overcome.

PLAYING RECORD

	Appearances	*Starts*	*Goals*
West Ham 1968–76	221 (178 in league)	213	58 (47 in league)
Tampa Bay Rowdies 1975 (loan)	19		6
Tampa Bay Rowdies 1976 (indoor and outdoor)	23		16
Feyenoord 1977–78	23		3
Portland Timbers (indoors and outdoors) 1977–81	124		40
Cleveland Force (indoors) 1979–80	30		33
Toronto Blizzard (indoors and outdoors) 1981–82	40		5
Los Angeles Lazers (indoors) 1982–84	90		29

HONOURS AND AWARDS

Year	Award
1998	Honoured at a dinner in Birmingham, England, as a pioneer of black footballers in England
2000	Received Queen's Certificate and Badge of Honour for services to football in Bermuda
2004	Received FIFA Order of Merit Award
2006	Received the MBE (Member of the Most Excellent Order of the British Empire) Award
2007	Inducted into Somerset Trojans Hall of Fame
2009	Awarded first place in Annual Caribbean Awards Sports Icons (CASI) 2013

ACKNOWLEDGEMENTS

GIVEN THE NUMBER OF PEOPLE I HAVE MET DURING MY FOOT-
ball career a list of all the names would be to long. First and foremost, I would
like to thank Dr. Derek Tulley and Mr. Jonathan Kent for encouraging me and
assisting me where needed, in getting this book underway. You both took a
journey and helped turn it into a story for many to enjoy. To all the people
that I have played for and against thank you because I could not have played
by myself. This include my first youth teams, Ireland Rangers, and West End
School. My high school team, my club team, Somerset Trojans, Triple Crown
Champs and Bermuda Youth and National Teams. All of these teams taught me
lessons to take onto WHUFC.

Secondly, there are my early coaches Ed "Ice Water" Smith, Hubby Rogers,
Earl Glasgow, Earl "Gabby" Hart, Conrad Symonds and especially, Graham
Adams. Thank you very much for being Bermuda's National Team Coach at
that time because without you God only knows what would have happened.

Thirdly, to my father and mother, Joseph and Dorothy Best, brothers, sisters,
uncles, aunts and cousins. Especially to my three cousins who I watched as a
young boy (Charles, Rudolph and Lionel) who all played for my club team
Somerset Trojans thank you very much for all you taught me. To all of the older
players in Bermuda playing during my younger years, you all played at such a
high standard that you all made me take it a step higher thank you again.

Fourthly, the Dexter family and then, Mrs. Charles, my mother away from home (may she rest in peace) her daughters Rita, Marg, Carol and sons John and Clive (may they rest in peace) and Bonzo and all of their children. Words cannot express the feelings I have in my heart for you all. To me you are and will always be my second family thank you to all of you.

Fifthly, Alan Olson, Frankie Mack, Terry Creasy, Georgie Kale, Big Al and Keith "the Comedian" friends that would never tell you "no" but would always say "yes". To the fans at WHUFC, thank you for your support that you gave me during my tenure their (I will always blow bubbles) and to the East End of London, my home away from home which will always be.

Lastly, to Ron Greenwood, John Lyle and Ernie Gregory (may they rest in peace). Where do I begin? Without the three of you there would be no book. You all saw me and you took a chance on a young boy from Bermuda. Thank you for the lessons you taught me on and off the field. I will be forever indebted to the three of you.

Finally, I would like to thank James Corbett and his team at deCoubertin Books for taking the initiative to publish this book and, of course, a big thank you to Andrew Warshaw for the countless hours and time he has put into this book.

IN THEIR OWN WORDS

Team-mates, opponents, supporters, managers and other players inspired by Clyde's story share their recollections of the great man.

CARLTON BEST

Older Brother

THERE ARE ONLY TWO YEARS BETWEEN US AND PEOPLE OFTEN used to think we were twins. We always had this love for football and used to kick a ball around with friends from the neighbourhood when we were kids and just got good at it. I was the rugged, hard-tackling type, Clyde was the gentlemanly one.

I'll never forget watching the West Ham–Preston FA Cup final with him and Clyde saying he was going to play for the Hammers. I never gave it much thought. Kids always say these kinds of things! But if truth be told, he was always going to play professionally. He did things instinctively and he used to kick the ball so hard. When he struck it straight at the goalkeeper's chest, you could see the guy wince!

I'm so pleased he achieved his dreams. We all are. I went to West Ham many times to watch him when I studied in south London. Then, as now, he was such an unassuming guy, down to earth and unboastful. He'd do anything for anyone . . . still does. Everyone back home loves him but you'd never know he was a football star: he's not a guy who stands out in a crowd. As a brother, he's been utterly dependable and even now comes to me for advice. I have a bakery and a deli in Bermuda and Clyde is my favourite visitor. I've always been his big brother – even though he's far bigger than I am!

*

PAT HOLLAND

Former West Ham winger and team-mate of Clyde

MY EARLIEST MEMORIES OF CLYDE WAS THIS GIANT BLACK GUY walking through the door at the West Ham training ground. Black players were pretty rare in those days and I always remember Bobby Moore looking up and saying how Clyde looked like a basketball player.

He made an immediate impact, not only in terms of his ability but also the fact that he was such a genuine fellow. He was really popular among everyone at the club. He was so modest and adapted so quickly to the English style despite walking into a brand-new social environment.

He got into the first team as a teenager and stayed there, unlike so many others. I think he was upset to have missed out on the cup final. Perhaps it was a catalyst for why he left.

Funnily enough, I saw him again in the 1970s when he was playing for Portland Timbers and I was playing for Team Hawaii. He still had it in bundles.

*

RONNIE BOYCE

Former West Ham midfielder, coach and team-mate of Clyde

IT COULDN'T HAVE BEEN EASY FOR CLYDE BECAUSE THERE WEREN'T many black players at the time. My first impression of him was what a lovely bloke he was. I know everyone seems to say that but that's how he came across. He used to speak his mind but it never ever got aggressive. He gave the opposition one hell of a hard time. He was big, strong, powerful and had a real eye for the goal.

*

SIR TREVOR BROOKING

Legendary West Ham winger and team-mate of Clyde

WHEN CLYDE FIRST ARRIVED AT WEST HAM HE WAS THIS BIG strong hulking lad who looked like a fully matured man, even though he was in the youth team. But his physique was in contrast to his character – totally laid-back and unassuming. You almost wanted to wrap him up in cotton wool.

It's important to point out that it was a time where being a black player had its obvious problems. There were plenty of people out there who wanted to make it difficult for him. He played at a time when black players were not prevalent and took quite a lot of stick verbally from opposition fans. But he dealt with it very well.

I think there were one or two occasions where he perhaps also struggled to lose weight, especially after he got married and started to enjoy home cooking! There were no sports scientists in those days, remember. But Clyde was totally dedicated to his task at hand and trained hard. He will always be remembered fondly by everyone he came into contact with at the club.

MICHAEL HART

London Evening Standard reporter and West Ham fan

HE WAS REALLY SHY, BUT WAS ALSO UNIQUE IN THAT HE WAS A high-profile black player – the most iconic black player in the game at that time, a mantle he never asked for and had to deal with. Then there was the fact there was another player around that time with the same surname!

I particularly remember the season West Ham had a marathon semi-final with Stoke. Bobby Moore went in goal when Bobby Ferguson got injured, even though Clyde was the number-one choice to serve as substitute goalkeeper. He was just too nervous about making a mistake, and who can blame him?

Once he opened up to the media, he was such an engaging bloke. I was quite surprised when I learned that back home in Bermuda he had become a prison officer. You'd never have guessed that's what he'd end up doing.

The West Ham fans loved him. He had this Sonny Liston look about him, a powerfully built centre-forward. Hursty loved playing with him. He thought the world of Clyde.

*

TERRY CREASY

Friend

I WAS A GOOD FRIEND OF ALL THE PLAYERS OF THE TIME – BOBBY Moore, Harry Redknapp, Frank Lampard, and so on. When he first came to West Ham, Clyde went to live at the Charles. family and I was a great friend of John.

When I went to Bermuda he thoroughly looked after me and my wife and i can only speak highly of him. The last time I saw him I told him he looked more like Archie Moore (the American boxer) than ever. He always contacts me when he comes over to the UK.

*

TONY COTTEE

Boyhood Hammer who followed Clyde as a West Ham forward

I COULD TALK ABOUT CLYDE BEST ALL DAY LONG.

My football memories begin in the 1972/73 season and although recollections are blurred from the very first game, I'm pretty certain Clyde would have been playing at Upton Park.

He was a hero of mine, one of the first players I became aware of as an elite sportsman. He stood out because he was a black player and there were very few black players around. He stood out also because of his ability. Clyde was a huge man, but a fantastic player as well.

I can't say I remember many individual games because I was too young. But my abiding memory of Clyde is seeing pictures of him in the famous away kit – a light-blue top with the two claret stripes. I can see him playing on a muddy pitch against Stoke City in the 1972 League Cup semi-final.

My dad was an avid West Ham fan and would speak fondly of Clyde and tell me how good a player he was.

I think it's fair to say back in the 1970s there was an undercurrent of vitriol that black players endured – it was a different world – and I think that was prevalent at all clubs. There was an emphasis on Clyde, a black player, playing for West Ham when no other team had any. And not only did West Ham have one, they had three or four in the team. Ade Coker and the Charles brothers, John and Clive, all played at the same time as Clyde. They had to put up with a lot of stick from opposing fans.

I can only imagine what it was like for Clyde and those boys. It was easier for me coming through as an eighteen-year-old, but Clyde being a black player, trying to break into the team and actually achieving it at the age of eighteen is a fantastic story and shows you what a good player he was.

He was a trailblazer.

I only met Clyde for the first time in my own retirement after football, but my opinion of him is: what a gentle giant, what a lovely, lovely person, and very humble man – someone you can talk to.

There's a real desire at West Ham to make sure the players that come through the youth system embrace the club's past. And if you're a sixteen- or seventeen-year-old breaking through now, I'm sure you'll know about Clyde.

STEVE MARSH

West Ham historian

TOWARDS THE END OF THE 1967/68 SEASON WEST HAM HAD contemplated disbanding their A Team and dropping out of the Metropolitan League for the upcoming campaign. However, the club revised their plans and stayed in the competition. To coincide with that decision South East Counties youth manager John Lyall took the next step on the managerial ladder for the Hammers by taking over the Metropolitan League side.

17-year-old Clyde Best arrived from his native Bermuda in the summer of 1968 for an extended trial period. The teenage striker made his initial debut in Lyall's Metropolitan League team against Bletchley on 17 August 1968.

Best is two years my senior, and I've always had an affinity with the big man: You could say we started our West Ham adventure together, Clyde the player and me a supporter. As Best was stepping onto the Manor Road Ground that August day, I was paying my two shillings and sixpence to go through the boys' entrance turnstiles on to the North Bank terracing at the Boleyn Ground to see my first-ever West Ham United game against Nottingham Forest.

Two months later I got my first glimpse of the youngster in person playing for the Reserves in a Football Combination fixture against Arsenal at Upton Park in October. From the very start you could see he was different from all around him, and not because of the colour of his skin. Although he was one of a handful of black players in the Football League at that time, the youngster stood out, standing over six-foot tall, this powerfully built striker towered over his colleagues and opponents. A week after watching him make his Combination debut he was representing Bermuda against the USA in a World Cup qualification in Kansas City.

At the end of his first season, Clyde had signed professional forms for the Hammers in April 1969 and with just 33 second and third-string games under his belt Best's elevation from the bone-hard pitches in his native Bermuda to the rain-sodden playing fields of the English Football League, playing alongside England's World Cup stars Bobby Moore, Martin Peters and Geoff Hurst was complete. That it had happened in little over a year was truly remarkable.

I, along with 39,590 others at Upton Park on 25 August 1969, witnessed his first team debut against Arsenal. Surprisingly for one so tall, he had a deft touch on the ground, he was quick to seize on any off chances that came his way and wasn't averse to helping out his defenders when called upon, the latter quite literally when he was called upon to deputise in goal for the injured Bobby Ferguson against Leeds United.

I was there to see his first goal in the 4-2 victory over Halifax Town in the League Cup. Although not a classic header he managed to deflected a Bobby Moore free kick with his head and into the goal.

Although he would be the first to admit that speed was not one of his strongpoints, that, along with his heading ability would come later with practice. However once mastered he was West Ham's top goal scorer for 1971/72 season with 23 goals and formed a formidable partnership with England striker Geoff Hurst which reaped 39 goals between them.

I've now completed my 48th season supporting the Hammers and in that time I've a hoard of memories. Clyde you are up there with the best of them and I thank you for contributing seven tremendous seasons to my memory bank.

*

IAN CALLAGHAN

Liverpool legend and record appearance holder who played against Clyde in the late 1960s and 1970s

I APPEARED IN 857 GAMES FOR LIVERPOOL, MORE THAN ANY other player in the club's history.

I hope you forgive me when I say that I do not remember them all. Football is relentless. There's a constant desire for success, especially at a club the size of Liverpool, with its huge history. You end up remembering the biggest moments: the important goals you scored, the finals and the trophies. I cherish those memories.

Yet in the course of a season, if you are competing on both domestic and foreign fronts, you regularly play between fifty and sixty games. Seasons, from one to the next, become blurred.

There are some opponents, though, you never forget. Inter Milan, Borussia Dortmund and Borussia Mönchengladbach. They roll off the tongue. Then there are players you played against many times. George Best and Bobby Charlton were two that stand out above the rest for their ability and presence.

If I think about West Ham United and their team in the 1960s, the obvious names enter my mind. Bobby Moore, in my opinion, is England's greatest defender. Then there was Geoff Hurst and Martin Peters: brilliant attacking players who I was fortunate enough to play with at the 1966 World Cup.

Clyde Best? There were few black players in the English First Division when he came from Bermuda. I'd played against Albert Johanneson at Leeds and Everton's Mike Trebilcock. It must have been hard for them because English football was an unforgiving place.

Clyde is up there among the toughest opponents I played against. He was fearless. Nothing seemed to bother him. Anfield, Liverpool's home ground, could be an intimidating venue and I witnessed a lot of good players crumble under the pressure.

Clyde certainly wasn't one of those players. He relished the challenge of trying to beat Liverpool, although I'm pretty sure our record against West Ham during Clyde's time there was pretty healthy.

Against Liverpool, Clyde would come across some of the most competitive defenders in English football. Initially, it would have been Tommy Smith and Ron Yeats. When Ron was sold Larry Lloyd came in and he, like Tommy and Big Ron, relished breathing down the neck of a striker.

After one game at Upton Park, I remember coming off the pitch at the end of a game, which finished as a 2–2 draw. Larry had endured a tough afternoon marking Clyde. 'He's tough as hell, that Best,' Larry kept saying.

And Clyde was.

*

GORDON TAYLOR

An opponent of Clyde as a Bolton and Birmingham City player; now the chief executive of the PFA

CLYDE WAS A GIANT OF A MAN, NOT ONLY IN STATURE BUT AS a role model for black footballers.

Black players were far from prominent when I was active as a footballer, for Bolton Wanderers and then Birmingham City, though I remember the general disgust among those I played with at the way some fans would react to fellow professionals like Clyde.

It wasn't until the late 1980s when attitudes really started to change and Clyde was a big part of that transition – one of the original pioneers. Players like Clyde, and Keith Alexander too, they changed those negative perceptions because of how they acted on the field, both as footballers and people.

I would say Clyde certainly paved the way for English football's very first black Player of the Year, John Barnes, in 1988.

Clyde stood out. I think it's fair to say he was a gentle giant in the mould of John Charles. And he could certainly play a bit too, in true West Ham style.

They were a good team in those days – like they're well known for, really: perhaps a little ahead of their time in regards to the attacking style that was implemented by Ron Greenwood. You always felt you were in for a good game and invariably came out having lost.

*

CLIVE TOYE

Former general manager of New York Cosmos, NASL commissioner and chairman of Toronto Blizzard during Clyde's spell at the club

ONE THING FOR SURE ABOUT CLYDE BEST IS THAT HE WAS WEL-come wherever he went – on the field or off it. At Toronto, he came in as the club was getting somewhere and he was starting to look towards the end of his playing career. Back in '72, one of his countrymen, Randy Horton (or, as he became, the Right Honourable K.H.R. Horton, minister of whatever), scored the winning goal when we, the NY Cosmos, won the league title.

Clyde didn't have a chance to do a repeat as it took us a couple of years to build properly. But the last time I saw him, I had to keep my distance . . . he was coach of Bermuda, playing a World Cup qualifier against the British Virgin Islands and I was the FIFA Match Commissioner, there to make sure that all was right and proper; a big smile was about as familiar as we could get.

*

DAVID FAIRCLOUGH

Former Toronto Blizzard team-mate

WHEN I SIGNED FOR TORONTO BLIZZARD, I DID NOT KNOW CLYDE Best was playing for them. Football was a much smaller world in 1982. So it came as some surprise when, waiting for the Toronto squad to arrive at a Vancouver hotel, he was the first one through the door.

I'd never been to North America before. I was frustrated by a lack of opportunities at Liverpool and was searching for something different. I knew very little about Toronto. The decision to move there was a new adventure, which excited me a lot.

Toronto had played a game in California and their representatives told me to meet them in Vancouver for the second leg of a run of fixtures on the west coast.

I was a bit nervous. Jimmy Nicholl, the Northern Irish former Manchester United centre-back, had moved there and though I'd played against him many times, I'd never met him socially. The Blizzard were a group of nomads: men who were either too young or too old to play in Britain or elsewhere and had chosen to take an alternative career path as a consequence.

I heard Clyde before I saw him because his laughter was so loud. It projected across rooms even if there were walls in between. He is such a bubbly character and it was clear to me from that first meeting in the Vancouver hotel that he was one of the leaders of the dressing room, along with Alan Merrick, the former West Bromwich Albion defender.

Clyde wasn't shy. My first couple of training sessions in Vancouver were on Astroturf pitches. It was raining heavily and I struggled to control the ball. I was slipping all over the place. The conditions were alien to me because in England all training and matches took place on grass. It prompted Clyde to christen me Bambi. Having spent eight years playing for West Ham United in the First Division, Clyde appreciated the dynamic of an English dressing room. Thankfully, on this occasion, the nickname did not stick.

While I was in Toronto, a player called Mark Hodder came over for a trial. Mark had been a youth player at Liverpool with me and he was a lively character. Clyde really liked Mark because his humour was typically Scouse.

Clyde was very settled at Portland before moving to Toronto and things did not really work out for him in Canada. Bob Houghton was the manager and he preferred to use a South African striker called David Byrne, who was short and tenacious. It resulted in Clyde featuring in exhibition matches while I was there, and I enjoyed playing with him. He was a true target man, someone who complemented my skill set, which was around pace and movement.

Clyde may have been frustrated but he never showed it. He was never quiet. He always tried to look at the positive and tried to be happy. His attitude was the right one to have in life.

JOHN PRATT

Former Portland Timbers team-mate

I FIRST KNEW CLYDE WHEN HE WAS AT WEST HAM AND I WAS AT Spurs. But we got to know each other better when both of us played at Portland in the United States.

He was a genuinely lovely, modest guy but he was street-wise with it. When I arrived and read a biography of all the players, I said, 'Bestie, I'm thirty-two now, how can you be twenty-eight? We played against each other as youth players.' He replied in his laid-back style, 'Easy, brother. There's another contract in there!'

To be serious, anyone who knows Clyde knows that he's a thoroughly nice man, a gentle giant. We had a unique situation at Portland. Everyone was mates. If someone had a barbecue, everyone was there. I think it was a breeding ground because everyone we signed, their wives soon became pregnant! Must have been a chair in the bar we used!

My main memory of Bestie in America is that he was a man for all seasons. No matter where we went he had a different accent depending on what part of the country we were in.

*

GARTH CROOKS

Former Stoke City and Tottenham forward and chairman of the PFA; now a well-known broadcaster.

I REMEMBER THE 1972 LEAGUE CUP SEMI-FINAL REPLAY BETWEEN Stoke City and West Ham United. I was at Old Trafford that day, supporting Stoke.

It was a very tense game and football fans in those situations – I suppose a lot like the players – will say anything they have to say to win the game. But Clyde handled that abuse like a giant. It didn't seem to affect him. He just dismissed it as what it was: Nonsense. Almost background noise.

But my goodness, that was when I realised that if I was going to survive as a black player in football I was going to have to have thick skin. Clyde showed that not only could it be done, it could be done with ease.

The thing about Clyde is he didn't just come and go, like some, he became very much a part of a football club's folklore and history at a time when it had never been done before. He was the most prominent black player of his generation. That's why people are so keen to talk about him.

Clyde had a standing, he had a presence that was dignified, and he behaved in a manner that black youngsters could embrace and feel proud of. He gave people a real sense of pride when they desperately needed it. In those days, black boys were leaving the game in their droves from the moment they entered the professional arena. But he encouraged an entire generation not to let this happen, to say: the abuse is not relevant; this is not part of our journey – unless you want it to be.

I watched a lot of Clyde's games on TV. I thought he was a terrific centre-forward. Though it was also my position, Clyde and I were very different players. He was this six-foot-two, strapping man. What he did extremely well was hold things up. He had good feet and when the ball came into him, it stuck. Positionally, he was as good as you got.

Yet the greatest impact he had on me was the way he brushed all his obstacles to one side. Perhaps, without seeing Clyde in that cauldron of Old Trafford all those years ago, and seeing how it could be done, I'd have been left with many more to overcome.

BRENDON BATSON OBE

Former Arsenal, Cambridge and West Brom full-back, and later a PFA official. Born in Grenada, like Clyde he was one of the first island footballers to break through in the English game

WHEN I ARRIVED AT ARSENAL AT THE AGE OF THIRTEEN I WAS very 9aware I was the only black boy on the team. In fact, I didn't come across many black players at all until I progressed to one of the top teams in the Regent's Park Sunday league.

Then, all of a sudden, Clyde Best burst on to the scene at West Ham. It's not so much me being inspired by Clyde, but almost like a journey we took together.

So when Clyde was coming through I was just relieved to see another black player. I remember he was this giant of a bloke: very strong, but very quick and very mobile. You'd see people trying to wrestle him down and he just used to plough through them. He scored some spectacular goals, too.

There was this aura about him and the papers were full of it. It would look very patronising now: 'Black Pearl' and 'Black Flash' and all that sort of stuff. But the profile he gained off the back of that served as encouragement to other black youngsters, who for the first time could look at football as a career, when a lot of black parents didn't want them to.

There was one guy I played with at Sunday level, who I thought was a really good player. He was on the books of Tottenham when I was at Arsenal, but the next thing I knew his parents had stopped him from signing and forced him to get a trade instead. So he became a spark, an electrician.

Around that time there were issues around immigration, you had the 'Rivers of Blood' speech from Enoch Powell, the National Front were quite active as well. Then there was the hooliganism and the abuse that was going on at grounds. You had to cope with a lot as a black player coming through. That's why parents were concerned. They'd say: 'How are you going to make a career: there's no one that looks like you?'

I don't recall having too much contact with Clyde, though I once bumped into him at Leyton Orient's ground, Brisbane Road, after we'd both gone to watch Laurie Cunningham play. It was all very random. I had nothing to do that day and Laurie, who I would go on to play with at West Bromwich Albion, was getting a bit of a profile as a youth player. So I went down to watch him, looked across the stand and Clyde was there doing the same thing.

It was around that time – the mid-1970s – that everything started to change. It was like a dam bursting and a load of black players came flooding through.

Clyde, along with Ade Coker and the Charles brothers with him at West Ham, were very much at the forefront of that movement.

*

NOEL BLAKE

Former Birmingham City and Portsmouth defender who was inspired by Clyde

I GREW UP IN BIRMINGHAM, ALTHOUGH I WAS BORN IN KINGSton, Jamaica. Throughout my childhood there was a football television programme in the Midlands called *Star Soccer*.

I remember Stoke City playing West Ham United. Clyde Best was West Ham's number 8 and the only black player on the pitch. He was so powerful and athletic. I wanted to be him.

I supported Birmingham City but I had a soft spot for West Ham because of Clyde. He was a scorer of terrific goals.

You tend to judge people by the company they keep and Clyde was in good company. The West Ham team included World Cup winners and he was trusted with what I believe to be the position on the pitch with the most responsibility. As a defender, I know how important the role of centre-forward is, and I think I can separate the good ones from the not so good ones.

Clyde certainly fell into the former category. As a Bermudian, he was the first iconic black player in the English game. He gave young black players more of a respect among professionals. He bore the brunt, paving the way so others could follow.

As an active black footballer in the 1980s with Birmingham, Portsmouth and Leeds United I became used to racist abuse from opposing fans. As a professional I had to develop an incredibly thick skin to remain and prosper in the game. It got to the stage where I entered the pitch expecting to be abused and, in some way, it inspired me to prove them wrong through my professionalism and performance.

At Portsmouth, I was often abused by small sections of my own supposed supporters and that hurt deeply. If you can't rely on the backing of those who are meant to want you to win, who else do you have to fall back on?

I realise that Clyde was subjected to similar treatment at West Ham and clearly he was able to brush it off and thrive regardless.

That demonstrates the courage of the man.

EXTRA TIME

∗

HOWARD GAYLE

*Liverpool's first black player, who went on to play for Newcastle, Sunderland,
Birmingham and Blackburn; like many of his generation, he considered
Clyde a role model*

I WAS NINE OR TEN YEARS OLD WHEN I SAW CLYDE BEST PLAY
football for the first time.

I was a black kid growing up in a white area of Liverpool and I suffered from
racist bullying while at school and on the streets.

I was also a massive Liverpool supporter and dreamed of representing the
club one day, although the ambition seemed unrealistic. There were few black
role models in the public eye.

Clyde, therefore, was a huge inspiration. His path towards First Division
football from Bermuda was unlikely and yet, he did it.

I viewed *Match of the Day* as a treat because it was on late every Saturday
after *Till Death Us Do Part*. My dad usually wanted me in bed way before it
started, so I'd hang around in the hallway hoping to hear the show's legendary
opening credits.

I'd plead with my dad to let me stay up and watch it. I loved Liverpool and
I idolised players like Roger Hunt and Ian Callaghan. Liverpool's games were
featured a lot because they, along with Manchester United, were emerging as the
leading forces in Britain.

The only other club that interested me was West Ham United and that was
purely because of Clyde, who led their forward line with great distinction, wearing the number 8 or 9 shirt.

Clyde was strong, athletic and fast. He often seemed to be getting the better
of defenders. He was a hero to West Ham supporters. His story proved to me
that if you want something and if you are talented – despite hurdles – you can
get to where you want to be if you are determined enough.

Much later, after three months in a young offenders' institute, I was eventually picked up by Liverpool after being spotted playing parks' football.

From there, it took me three years to reach Liverpool's first team, featuring in the squad that won the 1981 European Cup with victory over Real Madrid in Paris. By appearing against Manchester City at Maine Road earlier that season, I became the first black player to represent Liverpool in the club's history. Later, I played for England's under-21s while at Birmingham City before spells at Sunderland and Blackburn Rovers.

I often think back to my childhood and consider how it shaped me into the person I am now and the professional I became. Without the pioneering efforts of Clyde, maybe it wouldn't have been possible for someone like me to achieve my dream.

*

JOHN BARNES MBE

Legendary Liverpool and England winger and the first black PFA Footballer of the Year

IT IS A MISCONCEPTION THAT CLYDE BEST'S ACHIEVEMENTS reached out to every child in the Caribbean. First of all, Clyde came from Bermuda, and many people think Bermuda is in the Caribbean when it isn't. Although there are links both culturally and socially, geographically Bermuda is almost 2,000 miles to the northeast of the Caribbean islands.

I led quite a sheltered life in Kingston, Jamaica. My father was a high-ranking army official and we lived in a prosperous suburb. I was very, very fortunate.

I loved football but coverage of games in the English First Division was rare. If I close my eyes and think back as far as I can, the first match I remember on television involved the World Cup-winning West German national team of 1974. I was nearly eleven years old and I idolised Franz Beckenbauer.

I ended up spending most of my career at Liverpool and it is the city that has shaped me the most, but when I moved to England in 1976 after my father was promoted to the role of military attaché in London, I hadn't even heard of Liverpool. I guess I was naive. English culture was very different to what I was used to back home in Jamaica and the move was a huge one to make, one that would end up defining my life.

Clyde was coming to the end of his days as a West Ham United player at the time I arrived in England. A lot of my friends at school were Queens Park Rangers supporters so I started watching matches at Loftus Road. There were very few black players in the First Division, so when Clyde turned up, his presence took my eye.

London life was good to me. The Barnes family lived in a middle-class area and I certainly did not grow up with any self-worth issues. I was cosseted to a certain extent because I was not exposed to realities like other black kids.

That did not stop me thinking, though: thinking about how fortunate I was. I realised it was a difficult period to be a young black man in England, with the far-right making inroads in politics and attitudes towards black sportsmen usually prejudiced.

Clyde came to England a decade before me and laid foundations for black footballers in the professional game by playing so many times for one of the most historic clubs in the country and scoring so many goals.

Every black footballer has a lot to thank him for.

GARY BENNETT

Former Sunderland defensive stalwart inspired into professional football by Clyde

THERE WAS A TIME IN FOOTBALL WHEN, IF A PLAYER WAS BLACK, the first thing supporters would do would be to judge him by the colour of his skin rather than the shirt he was wearing.

I supported Manchester City and was a regular spectator at Maine Road as a teenager before enjoying a long playing career as a defender at Cardiff City and Sunderland, among other clubs.

I was a teenager in the mid-1970s when Clyde Best was coming towards the end of his spell at West Ham United. Then, football in England was a sport watched and played by white men.

The terraces at Maine Road were filled with white people. If a black player played for the opposition, he was going to get some stick. I was black and the environment was sometimes very uncomfortable. Ignorant attitudes were not restricted to Maine Road, though. As it was throughout society, racism was endemic in football.

Pelé and Eusebio were the first great black footballers with worldwide reputations. In England, Cyrille Regis, Laurie Cunningham and Brendon Batson came through together at the same time at West Bromwich Albion.

Clyde filled the gap in between. For a long period he stood alone as a high-achieving black player in the English game.

Having played at West Ham many times for Sunderland in the 1980s, I understand what a difficult place it can be to play, particularly if you were a black player not wearing the colours of West Ham. The terracing was close to the pitch and the atmosphere was intimidating. You'd notice few black faces. Attitudes towards minority groups were entrenched.

The club – and football – has travelled a huge distance since then, of course, but I imagine Clyde must have had to overcome a fair few trials and tribulations to achieve success.

Clyde stood out because of his skin but also because of his ability and his temperament. As a supporter, I watched him very closely and he always seemed in control of his emotions. Perhaps that helped him to deal with provocation.

His story taught me a lot. He proved that, through commitment and skill, you could change the attitudes of people even if they appear to be particularly dim when it comes to race.

Clyde was a pioneer.

HERMAN OUSELEY

Baron Ouseley of Peckham Rye, chairman of the Kick It Out campaign

CLYDE BEST IS A UNIQUE PERSON FOR ALL BLACK PEOPLE WITH an interest in football.

He assumed iconic status at a time when it was very exciting for black families to see a black person on television by virtue of the fact there were so few.

The fight goes on, but back in the 1960s and 1970s black people were fighting racism at every corner: in the workplace, in the job centres and on the streets. The colour bar existed still and that meant there were very few high-achieving black people, especially among the working class. Clyde's lonely presence at the very top of the game meant that he was a drop of water in a deep and wide ocean.

His success was also unusual because of his route into football. He came from Bermuda and made a huge name for himself at West Ham United – one of the most historic clubs in the old English First Division.

That unusual – improbable – route made black people believe that there were possibilities in life. I have no doubt that Clyde's achievements opened doors for black people, doors that were closed before his arrival on these shores.

Clyde was such a formidable-looking footballer. His size and strength was of Sonny Liston proportions, the famous boxer. And yet, he was also a cuddly bear. He never seemed to get ruffled. He was always relaxed. He confronted problems with a smile.

We could all learn from his story.

Q & A

In June 2016 readers from the *Knees Up Mother Brown* (kumb.com), a West Ham fans' website, were asked to submit their questions to Clyde. Here he answers the best of them.

. . . .

Where did you live while playing for West Ham? How did the neighbours treat you?

At first I lived at 23 Ronald Avenue with the family of John and Clive Charles. Everybody was great on the street – at least with me. At times, being a footballer can make you seem a bit special so we didn't ever have any problems. They might do something to your car if you parked it on their street, but they wouldn't do anything to mine. When I got married I moved to Pembroke Road, in Gants Hill – and that was nice! Nobody would touch your car there. But overall I'd say that people from the East End of London are some of the warmest you'll ever meet – I call that my second home – and I'll always be indebted to them.

. . . .

How did you feel when you arrived at Heathrow and nobody from West Ham was there, so you had to take a tube to Upton Park?

I understood . . . because I got the days mixed up! So I suppose I should take some of the blame as well.

. . . .

Do you realise the influence you had on so many young black men? And do you think your presence inspired more black players to come to West Ham?

I was always taught to think of those who come after you. I knew that I had a responsibility to behave myself and carry myself a certain way. And it gives me satisfaction when I hear so many people who say they're thankful for me. Nowadays, to see many players of colour playing, if I had something to do with it that's tremendous.

I think my presence certainly helped (to convince black players to come to West Ham). It was the first club in England to have three black players concurrently. So that was an obvious attraction, compared with other clubs. We were pioneers.

EXTRA TIME

• • • • • • •

What was it like playing under Ron Greenwood and John Lyall?

They were two very good coaches, who understood the game inside out, and they allowed us to play football. That's one thing about West Ham; we like to entertain the crowd, and they were two believers in that. They always preached it: We owed those fans; they paid their money to come and watch us. We were entertainers and we had to entertain them. I think the style they tried to implement was quite similar to what Slaven Bilic is doing now.

• • • • • • •

. . . And with some of the best players ever to wear the West Ham shirt?

Being in the company of some of the greatest players in the world, Bobby Moore, Geoff Hurst, Martin Peters, Trevor Brooking, Billy Bonds, was unbelievable. For someone from my little country – 22 square miles – to come there and play on the same stage as those guys was mind-boggling.

• • • • • • •

With all the talent in that side, why weren't more trophies won?

I think it's a lot to do with the way West Ham wanted to play. We played open, attacking football and most teams in England weren't doing that. When you want to play one way and everybody else another, that makes it difficult for you. We had some damn good players, and it would have been nice to win a cup or two, but it just wasn't to be at that time. We probably would have been better off today than we were then because more teams are choosing to play that way with a lot of coaches coming from the continent.

• • • • • • •

You were only 25 when you left for Tampa Bay Rowdies. At that age you would have been at the peak of your career, do you have any regrets about leaving the English First Division?

I could have done more there, yes. But I wasn't interested in playing for another club in England. I was West Ham through and through. The club gave me my first opportunity and they're my team. I perhaps didn't stay as long as I would have liked to, but I saw it as an opportunity to go to America and help to develop their programme. If you look at the growth of Major League Soccer in recent years, a lot of those who left England for America when I did played a big part in that. Nowadays they have purpose-built football stadiums, but when I was there they were using baseball stadiums; that's improvement.

• • • • • • •

How often do you visit West Ham?

I try to get back as often as I can. I wanted to come for the last game of the (2015/16) season but the flu interrupted me and I couldn't really travel. So I hope to come over this year; what with the book coming out and to see the new stadium. But I also get to see a lot of English football here in Bermuda; in fact, we probably get more than you do!

• • • • • • •

What is your view on the move to Stratford?

Of course, it's sad to leave Upton Park. The place had a real aura. I will always remember the closeness of the crowd. You could hear them shouting from the old chicken run; they would always let you know when you had a stinker! But we've got to move with the times and I think it's a good thing, overall. We'll get more people, more revenue, and we'll be able to attract better players. So hopefully, West Ham can finally challenge in the top four or five more often.

• • • • • • •

Do you have a favourite match for West Ham?

The first leg of the League Cup semi-final at Stoke (which was finally settled after 420 minutes). We beat them 2–1 and I scored a volley from Harry's cross. The next one was when we beat the great Leeds team (3–1) around Easter time (1974).

• • • • • • •

What was your best ever goal: away to Everton in 1972?

My best goal, or so John Lyall told me, was actually for the third team. I flicked the ball over the defender's head with the back of my heel and I volleyed it in the goal (laughs). But the one against Everton will take some beating, that's true. I ran the length of the field with the defender tagging on me, then when the goalkeeper came I sold him a dummy and clipped it over his head. What made it better was the crowd making monkey chants – being the only black player I knew they were for me – so to go and silence them was brilliant.

· · · · · · ·

Who was the toughest defender you played against?

They were all tough in those days. Ron Harris, Norman Hunter . . . Big Jack (Charlton) would give you a boot now and again. But being a big person helped me tremendously. It didn't bother me playing against people like that.

· · · · · · ·

Do you remember shoulder-charging Tommy Smith and knocking him flying?

Yes, I remember; he tried to hit me and ended up on his backside! I was still eighteen or nineteen then and probably shocked Tommy a bit because he was known as a hard fella, but I got to know him over the years because he came to Tampa Bay Rowdies.

· · · · · · ·

Do you still keep in touch with your former team-mates? Who?

When I go back I always try and catch up with somebody. I usually see Frank (Lampard Snr), I've spoken to Pat Holland, Tony (Carr), I speak to Paul Heffer a lot. Last time was good because I got to see Boycey (Ronnie Boyce), who I hadn't seen for ages; Ken Brown, Peter Brabrook. But that's West Ham; it's a friendly club where everybody gets along from the tea lady to those in the boardroom. That's what I'll always remember. The last people I saw from the old team were Harry (Redknapp) and Frank(Lampard), I was trying to get Trevor (Brooking) here for a golf tournament but he couldn't do it. I'll see if I can get him next year instead.

A lot of fans who come here will try and contact me and I'll do my best to go and see them. I've just taken a guy on a tour today and he brought me a shirt from the final game of the season. I was glad to get that, I'm going to frame it and everything!

INDEX